SPIRITS &
LIQUEURS

by Rosalind Cooper

© 2010
White Mule Press
Box 577
Hayward, CA 94541
www.distilling.com

ISBN
978-0-9824055-7-4

Contents

Introduction

Spirits and liqueurs have a long history in many of the world's cultures. At first they were mainly used as medicines and tonics. Now they're flavorful social beverages enjoyed at home or in the friendly atmosphere of a bar or restaurant.

Choose from an exciting selection of both domestic and international spirits and liqueurs. This immense variety can be confusing when you're trying to find the drink that suits your mood or a special occasion.

This book helps you make the right decisions. It provides a clear and simple guide to the world's selection of spirits and liqueurs, so you can choose among them confidently. It offers suggestions on how to serve these beverages—straight *(neat)* or in mixed drinks.

You'll find recommendations of appropriate glassware for different types of spirits. Selected recipes for classic cocktails help you prepare your drinks with elegance and skill.

Many people miss out on the diverse adventure of spirits by confining themselves to a few well-known drinks. You don't have to! With this book you'll discover some intriguing concoctions—both exotic and familiar ones.

The entire assortment of spirits has this in common: They're beverages of high alcoholic strength distilled from beverages of lower alcoholic strength. The majority, including whiskeys, are based on a "beer" made from a grain such as rye or barley. Brandies, on the other hand, are distilled from a wine that has been fermented from grapes or other fruits.

Liqueurs are made of spirits combined with a sweetener and various flavors and colors. The exact constituents of each liqueur are a closely guarded trade secret. This secrecy is not just a commercial necessity but dates back to the era when liqueurs were reputed to cure diseases or mend broken hearts.

Although we don't believe in such all-healing powers today, spirits and liqueurs are still regarded as special. A lot can be said for the warm personal communication that comes from sharing a well-made drink. There's no mysterious talent to serving a perfect highball, cocktail or cordial—it's merely a matter of knowing how.

In the pages that follow, you'll learn all you need to know about carefully choosing and graciously serving a wide variety of spirits and liqueurs. Use them to toast special occasions or add a touch of ceremony to everyday life. In both circumstances, I wish you happy drinking.

The Story of Spirits

Woodcut illustration from *The Books of the Alchemy of the Most Ingenious Arabian Philosopher, Geber* printed at Berne, 1545.

There's an air of mystery, myth and even magic, surrounding the history of distillation. Throughout the ages, both spirits and liqueurs have possessed legendary qualities, with a reputation for prolonging life, curing ills and warding off disease.

ORIGINS AND HISTORY

It's uncertain exactly where or when the notion of distilling wine or other fermented beverages originated. Most likely, the idea was independently discovered in cultures around the world. There's evidence that the ancient Egyptians knew about distillation. Chinese writings mention the extraction of strong spirits from fermented rice as early as 1000 B.C. A bit later, natives of the East Indies learned to distill potent alcohol from a similar rice-and-sugar wine.

The general principles of boiling a liquid to extract its essence were widely known in ancient Greece and Rome. Aristotle mentions a "wine that produces a spirit." Both Hippocrates and Galen recommended using a concentrated essence of wine to dress wounds and purify water. In Latin, spirits are know as *aqua vitae*, or *water of life.*

In the eighth century A.D., an Arab alchemist known as Geber wrote a lengthy treatise on the distillation of spirits from wine. He performed his experiments in a vessel called an *alembic*, a metal heating container with a tube that led to a separate cooling chamber. In their conquest of Spain, Geber's Moorish colleagues introduced this clever distilling device to Europeans. Design improvements eventually led to the pot still, which continues to be used today.

The secret of distillation spread rapidly. In 1310, a French chemist named Villanova detailed the process and called its product "the golden water that strengthens the body and preserves life."

Medicinal uses of spirits continued throughout medieval times. When the Black Death ravaged Europe in the mid-14th century, many physicians prescribed spirits both as tonics and purifiers of drinking water. The great religious houses manufactured spirits as a base for flavored cordials, the forerunners of today's liqueurs and after-dinner drinks.

Gradually, the skill of distillation passed from the control of monks and doctors to private winemakers and brewers. When grape harvests were poor in France, enterprising winemakers converted low-quality wines into delicious brandies.

Distillation of spirits from grain or potatoes may have an even longer European history than distillation of brandy from wine. According to legend, St. Patrick taught the Irish how to make *potheen* from malted barley, thus establishing the principles for making whiskey.

By Shakespeare's time, all Northern European countries had learned to produce their own starch-derived spirits. Scandinavians gained a reputation as heavy drinkers with their potato-based *aquavit*. The nearby Dutch preferred juniper-flavored Genever gin, consumed straight and chilled. An unflavored version of this drink originated in Russia, where it was called *vodka.*

In Britain, brandy was the fashionable drink; imports from France were substantial. Parisians were so partial

An engraving of a distillery and laboratory, 1748.

to it that vendors sold it in small glasses from pushcarts on the streets. The English word *brandy* is shortened from the Dutch term *brandewijn,* meaning burnt wine.

Early settlers in the New World sought to ease their harsh pioneer life with spirits fermented and distilled from wild fruits and vegetables. Early "moonshine" spirits made with corn or rye are the ancestors of today's American whiskeys. On the sea-trading routes between Europe and America, mariners grew fond of a full-flavored drink called *rum,* which originated in the sun-drenched islands of the Caribbean.

Back on the shores of England, a major change in drinking habits was taking place. Soldiers returned from 16th century religious wars in Holland with a taste for Dutch courage—strong, cold Genever gin. Gin soon became the drink of choice in English taverns! Despite legal attempts to control its local production, the quality of this cheap spirit was often very bad. Hogarth's paintings of Gin Lane are all too accurate in their depiction of the drunken misery gin caused the poor of London.

Among wealthy classes, spirit-drinking was equally widespread on both sides of the Atlantic. Many ladies of the 18th century enjoyed "sylla-bubs" liberally laced with gin or rum. Sweetened cordials and liqueurs

became fashionable, often taken as *digestives* after rich meals.

The social turmoil of the Industrial Revolution brought further proliferation of cheap spirits, especially in the cities. Reformers did their best to improve the quality of the spirits sold, but legislation did little to help control abuses.

MODERN TIMES

At the end of the 19th century, blended Scotches appeared for the first time. These lighter-tasting spirits became an acquired taste with U.S. soldiers returning from Europe after World War I. Soon zealous lawmakers noticed that alcohol consumption was generally on the increase across the United States. The Volstead Act of 1919 actually banned the production and consumption of alcoholic beverages, producing the period popularly called *Prohibition.*

Ironically, Prohibition led to even greater popularity of spirits of all kinds, although quality was variable on the bootleg market. The unpleasant flavor of ill-made spirits was often masked by mixers. Thus the cocktail became a symbol of the Jazz Age.

At the same time, a demand arose for imported brand-name spirits, such as Gilbey's gin and Cutty Sark Scotch. Drinkers chose well-known labels to get reliable quality. After Prohibition was lifted, people remained loyal to these brands. Sales of imported Scotch and gin became enormous.

The Second World War also brought thousands of U.S. troops to Europe. This time the drinking influence worked both ways—U.S. soldiers enjoyed Scotch and French brandy, and at the same time introduced Europeans to American bourbon and rye whiskeys.

Since the war, brand names became more important. Huge international companies now spend large sums to promote their particular spirits and liqueurs. The modern drinker seems to appreciate less strong-flavored, lighter-bodied styles—notably white rum, gin and vodka. The notorious cocktail of Prohibition days has gained new respectability and popularity.

Yet the associations of distilled spirits with magic and medicine are not lost. Many claim that a little drink after dinner helps digestion. Some people have a special bottle of brandy tucked away for medical emergencies.

Basics of Distillation

The process of distillation is making liquids of high alcoholic strength from liquids of lower alcoholic strength. The original Latin verb *destillare* means 'to trickle down', like raindrops on a window or condensed steam on a glass coffeepot.

During distillation, a base liquid containing alcohol is heated until the alcohol becomes a steam, or vapour. Because alcohol boils at a lower temperature than water, it is possible to vaporize nearly all the alcohol in the base liquid, leaving mostly water behind.

The vapour is trapped and cooled, so it condenses back to a liquid state. The resulting liquid has a higher concentration of alcohol. This process gives us the word *spirit* – the liquid seems to come out of the air.

Distillation sounds easy, and so it is, if you are making industrial-grade alcohol. However, producing a safe and good-tasting alcoholic beverage is much more delicate and complex.

DISTILLATION STEPS

Spirits are made in specially designed machines called *stills*. As the base liquid in the still warms up, the first vapour that forms is methyl alcohol. This is the type of alcohol used in substances such as fuel and antifreeze. It's lethal stuff. Modern distillation methods first remove all of the methyl alcohol.

After all of the vaporized methyl alcohol is removed, ethyl alcohol – the alcohol in the spirits you drink – begins vaporizing along with some water. The vaporized mixture is carefully collected by rapid condensation until the later stages of distillation, when it becomes more water than alcohol. Typically, distillers must re-distil the base liquid at least once and sometimes three or four times.

Besides alcohol and water, base liquids contain many other aromatic and flavourful elements called *congeners*. These add richness and complexity to a finished spirit. It's the distiller's challenge to capture them without including any undesirable impurities present.

If the spirit is to have a neutral taste, as in vodka and gin, the condensed vapour – called the *distillate* – must be re-distilled, or *rectified*, after collection. Rectification is simply a technical term for repeated distillations that remove all traces of flavour from the pure spirit.

TWO STYLES OF SPIRIT

To classify the varied spirits of the world, you should consider this – does this spirit have its own intrinsic flavour, or is it a neutral spirit with added flavours? To understand the difference, consider brandy and gin.

Brandy is derived from the fermented juice of grapes or other fruit. This basic wine has a multitude of flavours, many of which remain in the spirit after distillation. In addition, the young spirit is transferred to wooden casks for ageing, and the wood lends flavour and colour to the finished product.

On the other hand, gin is made from rectified spirits that can be distilled from a variety of base materials, including grains, potatoes and molasses. In fact, when gin was the most popular spirit of the English public, Scottish whisky was used for rectifying into gin.

After rectification, the gin spirit has no flavour except for the taste of the alcohol it contains. At this stage, distillers add herbs such as juniper and coriander to give gin its distinctive character.

TYPES OF STILLS

The pot still is the traditional tool of the distiller. Its basic design has changed little since the days when medieval monks distilled spirits for medicinal purposes. It's usually made of copper in the shape of an onion.

Even today the pot may be heated by a fire burning below it. More often, however, it is encircled by gas-operated warming coils. The heated liquid inside the still vaporizes and passes through a spout to a condenser, where the spirit is liquified and collected. The process is slow because only small quantities are made at one time in each pot still.

Today, pot stills are used for higher-priced spirits known for their special rich flavours. These include malt Scotches from Scotland, Cognac brandy from France, Irish whiskeys and most dark rums. They may also be used for rectification in making gin or other 'white' spirits.

The patent still – also called the *continuous* or *Coffey* still – was invented in 1831 by Aeneas Coffey, an Irishman. It can be used almost continuously, day and night, without the constant attention required by a pot still. Here's why: a steady stream of liquid enters the still at the top of a copper column, where it is heated to steam and vaporized. The distillate then passes through condensing coils into another column, where it is re-vaporized by steam and rectified. Specially designed plates inside the still ensure that the correct proportions of drinkable elements are collected.

The advantages of this system are many. Large quantities of spirits are produced at relatively low cost. In addition, the patent still is more successful at purifying alcohol than the pot still. Most modern drinkers prefer a light type of drink – a speciality of the patent still.

Depending on how often the spirit is passed through the still, the end product may taste neutral like vodka or have much flavour, like grain whiskies. With the patent still, a famous brand of spirit may be made anywhere in the world. The product of the pot still depends on the local water and other specific operating conditions for its unique flavour.

DETERMINING ALCOHOL STRENGTH

The final distilled spirit is part liquid alcohol and part flavoured water. People like to know how strong the spirit is in terms of alcohol percentage. The simplest measuring system is called *Gay Lussac* (G.L.), after a famous French physicist. The G.L. system measures the percentage of pure alcohol in a given volume of wine or spirit on a scale from 0% (pure water) to 100% (pure alcohol). On a bottle that contains 40% alcohol, for example, the label will say 40% G.L.

British and Americans also use the word *proof* to denote alcohol strength, but they determine it differently. In the U.S., the proof value is twice the alcohol strength. For example, 100 U.S. proof equals 50% alcohol by volume (50% G.L.). But we use a different scale. For a clear comparison, see the accompanying table.

Prior to 1816, a spirit's strength was measured by mixing it with gunpowder. If the concoction exploded when touched with a match, this was 'proof' of its potency. Fortunately, today we measure proof more scientifically with an instrument called a *hydrometer*.

BOTTLE SIZES

Spirits commonly come in three sizes of bottles – 750 millilitres (25.4 fluid ounces), 1 litre (33.8 fluid ounces) and 1.75 litres (59.2 fluid ounces). You can also buy pint and half-pint sizes. The sizes of liqueur bottles are more varied, but the amount is in metric volume measure on the label.

STORAGE

Although spirits and liqueurs do not deteriorate with storage as readily as fine wines, they do lose some of their subtle flavours and alcohol when kept in an unsealed bottle. If you plan to use a certain beverage only occasionally, it's wise to purchase it in a small bottle.

In a pot still, the wine or cereal mash is put in the pot and heated. The resultant vapour passes through a coiled tube in a water-cooled condenser, where it becomes liquid. It's collected in a barrel.

The Pot Still

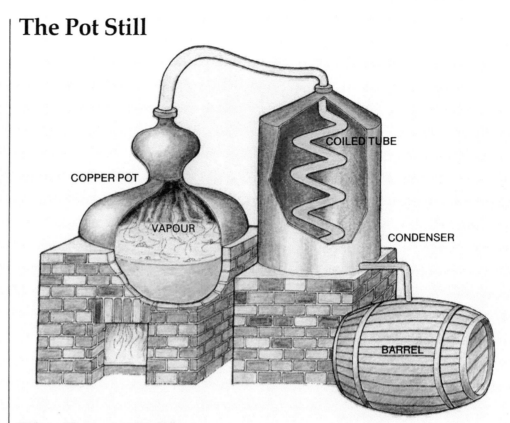

The Patent Still

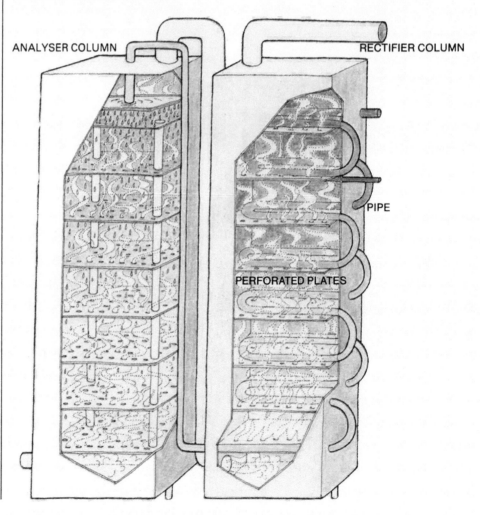

MEASURES OF ALCOHOLIC STRENGTH		
% G.L.	U.K. Proof	U.S. Proof
10	11.50	20
20	35	40
30	52.50	60
40	70	80
41	71.75	82
42	73.50	84
43	75.25	86
50	87.50	100
57.14	100	114.28
60	105	120
70	122.50	140
80	140	160
90	157.50	180
100	175	200

In a patent still, the wash enters the rectifier and descends through a twisted pipe heated by steam coming up through perforated plates. It is then fed into the top of the analyser. At the bottom, the alcohol is evaporated and passes over to the rectifier where, as it rises, it condenses into spirit that is drawn off near the top.

Spirits

Whiskey

The staff at the famous Glenlivet distillery in 1924.

In the United States the word *whiskey* means only U.S.-distilled bourbons and blends. In fact, Scotland's smoky-flavored Scotch and Canada's mellow rye are also members of the whiskey family. Japan, Australia and many other countries also pride themselves on their own versions of this full-bodied drink.

There's no question that the Scots produce some of the world's finest whiskeys. Rare and expensive *single malts* are made by an age-old process in the Scottish Highlands. In the same price bracket are the deluxe blended Scotches, which have loyal followings.

But when it comes to an everyday whiskey mixed with soda or made into another long drink, other world whiskeys pose stiff competition to Scotch. The light-bodied Canadian and American rye whiskeys are often the choice of the modern drinker. In fact, the world's top-selling brand of whiskey, Seagram's 7 Crown, is American.

COMMON CHARACTERISTICS

What do all these whiskeys have in common? The answer is that they're based on cereal grains, such as barley, that are fermented to use as a base for the distilled spirit. Beyond this point, the secrets and mystique of whiskey making take over. Each producer has a special recipe and technique for his particular product.

WHISKY AND WHISKEY

You may wonder why some whiskeys are spelled with an *e* and some without. Scotch whisky (*pl.* whiskies) is spelled without the *e* because Scottish exporters want to clearly distinguish their product. Canadian distillers have followed suit.

Irish manufacturers prefer their whiskey (*pl.* whiskeys) with an *e*, as do most Americans, although the U.S. Bureau of Alcohol, Tobacco and Firearms omits it in their standards. This book respects the Scottish and Canadian preference when refering to their whiskies, but uses the *e* to refer to all other whiskeys.

HISTORY

The Irish and the Scots have long fought over the question of who first distilled strong spirits. The word *whiskey* is derived from the Irish Celtic term *uisgebaugh* or the Scottish Celtic *uisgebeatha*. Both words mean *water of life,* indicating how much the Celts liked their drink.

Despite Scottish insistence to the contrary, many chroniclers of whiskey agree that Irish monks probably began it all. From Ireland, the secret spread to Scotland via missionary monks who settled in the Highlands.

The Scots took to the idea with enthusiasm. As visitors to this lovely country have discovered, its beauty is often contrasted by the ferocity of its climate. Like the Scandinavians with their aquavit, the Scots used their whisky to help ward off the bitter chill. The 18th-century writer Tobias Smollet recorded how Scotch was commonly used as "an excellent preservative against the winter cold," but Scots were not averse to a "wee dram" at any season.

When Samuel Johnson visited Scotland, he noted, "As soon as he appears in the morning, a man of the Hebrides swallows a glass of whisky." He also observed that the locals rarely seemed drunk.

Almost every Scots nobleman had his own still, and he generously distributed the pungent spirits to his entire household. In town and cities, neighbors shared distilleries. In 1777, more than 400 illegal stills were discovered in Edinburgh alone.

During the 18th century, Scotland was a relatively wild and inhospitable place. Successive governments in London tried to impose taxes on alcohol-making, but tax collectors found it nearly impossible to enforce these laws. So-called "smugglers" would pack up and move their stills as soon as the tax man came near. Illicit distilling was not effectively stamped out until 1814.

This stubbornness is similar to that of U.S. settlers who moved inland from the coastal towns to wilderness areas such as Bourbon County, Kentucky. Because corn was a dietary staple, corn liquor was their strong drink—a whiskey known today as *bourbon*. Another well-known American whiskey, rye, is made mostly from that grain. This spirit is generally associated with the Northern states, just as bourbon is with Kentucky and the South.

The first Canadian distillers were immigrants from Scotland. Although Canadian whisky is also made with rye, other grains are added to the rye in a variety of proportions that vary in each distillery.

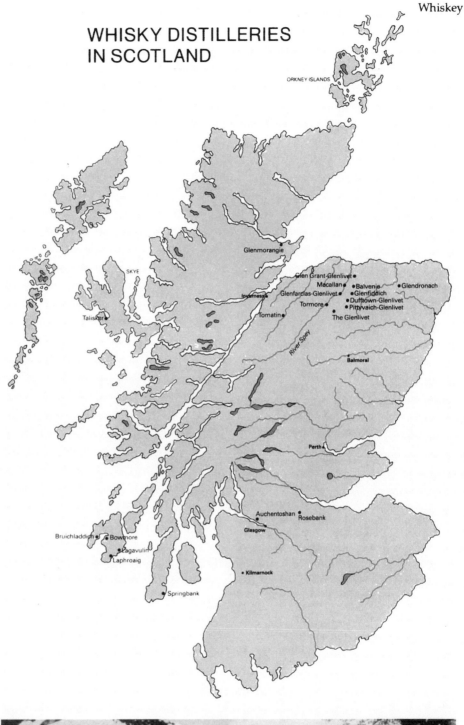

WHISKY DISTILLERIES IN SCOTLAND

The Glendronach malt whisky distillery, owned by Wm. Teacher and Sons.

HOW WHISKEY IS MADE

By the early 19th century, whiskeys had established a popularity in their various areas of production, but almost none were exported from Europe or North America. Because the pot still was used, the process was long and elaborate. There wasn't enough surplus product for export.

In 1831 the Coffey still—also called the *patent* or *continuous* still—revolutionized spirit making. As a result of the new continuous process, a whole new style of beverage was developed. Before this time, the pot still had given all whiskeys a powerful and distinctive flavor that was often smoothed by *blending* different spirits. High-proof drinks were actually strong enough to burn the tongue.

The product of the continuous still is lighter, smoother and lacks some of the characteristics of pot-still whiskey, but it can be made in huge amounts at relatively low cost. In Scotland, full-flavored malt whiskies continue to be produced by the traditional pot-still process, but blended whiskies are dominant. Scotch blends are made up of some malt whisky subtly combined with patent-still whiskies made from various cereal grains to give a blander taste.

Unlike Scotches and Irish whiskeys, unblended, straight U.S. whiskeys are made exclusively by the patent-still process. They resemble Irish whiskeys insofar as they are distilled from a mash made from a variety of grains. After aging, nothing is added but water.

POT-STILL WHISKEY

Barley is the essential ingredient for traditional malt Scotch and Irish whiskeys. This particular grain has a special property—it can convert its own starch into sugar. Sugar is needed for fermentation to create the alcohol that is distilled into whiskey.

Malting—The barley is moistened and spread on a warm floor. As the seed begins to grow, it becomes *malt*, or germinated grain. Starch in the seed converts to *maltose*, a type of natural sugar. When the shoots are almost an inch long, they are dried over fires at high temperatures. The Scots use peat fires to give their whiskies a special smoky aroma. In Ireland, coal fires are used, and the barley is later mixed with other cereals.

Fermentation—This process is similar to that used in beer making. The dried malt is ground into a meal, or *grist*, then mixed with hot water in large vats called *mash tuns*. When the water has absorbed all the goodness of the grain, it is known as *wort*. Yeast is added to consume sugars and give off its byproducts of carbon dioxide gas and liquid alcohol. Due to the gas, the wort bubbles fiercely as it ferments, giving off the characteristic yeasty smell.

Distillation—The fermented wort, really a form of beer, goes into the wash still for its first distillation. It is re-distilled into spirit in another gleaming copper pot still. Irish whiskeys are re-distilled yet a third time to give them their characteristic smoothness.

Maturation—The pure spirit, colorless and fiery, is transferred to old, used wooden casks for maturation. For Scotch, the minimum aging period is three years. This allows the wood to give the spirit a brown color and nutty flavor. Casks used for aging malt whiskey are traditionally those first used for sherry. However, because sherry is more frequently shipped in bottles these days, many Scotch and Irish distillers are now using old American bourbon casks. Used barrels are employed to avoid too strong a wood flavor in the finished spirit.

PATENT-STILL WHISKEY

Almost all the world's whiskeys are made with this kind of still. They are based on a mixture of grains like corn, rye, wheat and barley. The exact proportions of each grain in the grain *mash* are well-guarded company secrets, giving each brand a characteristic taste.

The first steps in the patent-still method are similar to those used in traditional pot-still production. When the grain arrives at the distillery, it is carefully inspected and washed. It is then taken to the gristmill to be ground into a meal.

Cooking The Cereals—The ground grains are mixed with hot water and pressure-cooked. Cooking releases the starches from their tough outer seed coats. The liquid wort is then transferred to a mash tun, as in the pot-still process.

Fermentation—At this stage, the cooked cereals are rapidly cooled and mixed with ground malted barley, which acts on the other cereals to convert their starches to sugars. Pure cultured yeast is added, and fermentation occurs, as described.

Distillation—The fermented beer goes into the patent still for distillation and rectification. Depending on the type of whiskey, proof will vary from 140 to 160 at this stage.

Maturation—The new spirit passes to casks for aging. Scotch must be aged for a minimum of three years. Other world whiskeys require a similar aging to become smooth.

BLENDING AND FINISHING

Less than 2% of all exported Scotches are sold as distinctively smoky-flavored single malts. The rest are mixed with grain-based Scotches to achieve a smoother, lighter character. Scotches are classified as "popular" if they contain about 15% malt spirit to 85% grain. More expensive, deluxe blends have a much higher proportion of single-malt spirit. Fuller in body and flavor, they are particularly popular in Eastern U.S. cities.

Up to 50% of all U.S.-distilled whiskeys are sold as straight, or *unblended*, spirits. The rest are mixed with other whiskeys before they're put in casks for aging. All Canadian whiskies are blended, as are many of the other world whiskeys.

The blender is a highly skilled person who makes his selection from up to several dozen different ingredients. They may include grain whiskeys, grain neutral spirits, and high-proof spirits known as *light whiskeys*. Some blenders also add special flavorings like sherry wine or fruit juice.

All distillers add pure water to their whiskeys to reduce the proof, either before aging or before bottling. Local waters lend uniqueness to individual whiskies.

Some of the tawny color of a whiskey comes from aging in wooden casks. Usually, however, the distiller deepens the color with a small amount of caramel.

Aged and colored spirit is clarified for bottling by filtration through charcoal or other porous materials. Some imported brands are shipped across the Atlantic in bulk and bottled in the United States to save duty and taxes.

Top: The traditional barley-malting method is to let it germinate on the malting floor.

Bottom: Stoking the peat kiln to dry the malted barley.

Right: Malt-whisky pot stills. All photographs courtesy of the Glendronach distillery.

MALT WHISKEY

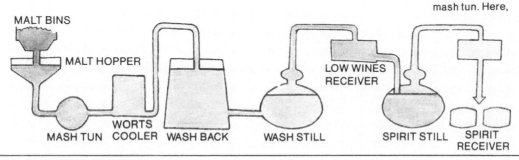

MALT BINS

MALT HOPPER

LOW WINES RECEIVER

WORTS COOLER

MASH TUN WASH BACK WASH STILL SPIRIT STILL SPIRIT RECEIVER

To become malt whiskey, malted barley is first fed into the hopper and transferred to the mash tun. Here, thorough mixing with spring water takes place to form the *wort*. This is fed into the wash back where yeast is added to produce an alcoholic *wash*. The first distillation produces low wines that are pumped into the pot still. After re-distillation, the new whiskey is put in cask where it matures for at least 3 years.

GRAIN WHISKEY

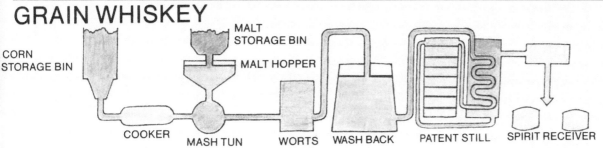

MALT STORAGE BIN

CORN STORAGE BIN

MALT HOPPER

COOKER MASH TUN WORTS COOLER WASH BACK PATENT STILL SPIRIT RECEIVER

To become grain whiskey, corn is fed into the cooker where it mixes with hot water, and is then drawn off into the mash tun. Malt is fed into the mash tun and converts the corn starch to sugar. The wort passes into the wash back where yeast is added. This is then passed through a patent still and the resulting spirit is collected in casks for maturing.

Right: Skilled blenders testing a sample of Johnnie Walker Whisky.

Above: Casks being made at the Johnnie Walker cooperage at Kilmarnock.

17

SCOTCH BLENDS

To a Scotsman, the word *whisky* is synonymous with the peat-smoked beverage of Scotland. He'd never call it *Scotch*. Others, however, use the word *Scotch* to mean Scottish whiskies exclusively.

The history of blended Scotch is only about 100 years old. During the 1880s, all of Europe's vineyards were attacked and killed by a louse that gnawed the roots of the vines. Wine production was virtually halted until Americans came to the rescue with native vine stocks that were resistant to the louse.

Because the vines were destroyed, the production of French brandy from wine also stopped. Spirit drinkers had to find an alternative. They turned to Scotch, although it had no big reputation at the time. The heavy pot-still malt Scotches were considered too powerful for everyday drinking, unless of course you were actually in the cold climate of the Scottish Highlands.

Two factors combined to help Scotch become more popular. One was the sheer determination of pioneer Scotch salesmen like James Buchanan and Tommy Dewar. The other was the development of a whole new style of spirit—the grain-and-malt blend.

People were accustomed to drinking their brandy mixed with soda or water. To make Scotch a suitable substitute for this purpose, the distillers had to come up with a lighter style. They achieved this by blending a high proportion of grain whisky from a patent still with a quantity of full-flavored malt whisky. Thus began such popular brands as Black & White, Dewar's White Label and Johnnie Walker Red Label, all of which are still made.

In the United States, interest in blended Scotch really began after World War I. But it was during the 14 years of Prohibition that Scotch sales really boomed. British merchants had large stocks in the Bahamas which were sold to bootleggers for "export," eventually arriving at *speakeasies*.

Scotch could be obtained legally if you had a doctor's prescription for it. The *Saturday Evening Post* commented in 1921, "A nation that has developed enough sickness in eight months to require 18 million gallons of whisky to alleviate its suffering may be depended on to remain sick indefinitely." Once Tommy Dewar was visiting a dry state when someone suggested that he try a special cholera medicine. Imagine his surprise when he discovered that it was none other than a bottle of his own famous blend!

A great deal of the whiskey for sale in illegal bars during Prohibition was of poor quality. Demand for a reliable supply of good liquor was becoming almost desperate. Soon a Scotch whisky merchant named Francis Berry, of the old London export house of Berry Brothers & Rudd, determined to meet this demand. He made contact with a notorious mariner, one Captain William McCoy.

Berry asked him what, in his opinion, was the style of whiskey Americans and Canadians really enjoyed. McCoy's reply carried great weight, as he had a reputation for carrying only the best product—the "real McCoy." He recommended the blending of a "light blend, with a light aspect," like a pale sherry. The result of this conversation was the first shipment of Cutty Sark Scotch, setting a new style that became popular.

In the 1980s, both Dewar's and Cutty Sark are still among the favorite brands in the United States, in addition to J&B, another light style. Such brand loyalty is what the exporters of blended Scotch want. It's the reason they spend large sums both on advertising and on promoting sporting and cultural events worldwide.

GOOD SCOTCH BLENDS

More than 2000 brands of Scotch are produced for sale in the British market alone, with a much higher total when export brands are included.

Despite the extensive choice, the bulk of sales are controlled by a few firms. Largest is the Distillers Company Ltd. (DCL). This company owns about 40 malt distilleries. The majority of the production from these goes into their famous blended Scotches, including John Haig, Johnnie Walker, Black & White, Dewar's White Label, White Horse and VAT 69. Distiller's Company products account for half of all exports of Scotch—and 85% of total Scotch production is exported.

The following is a brief guide to some excellent brands of Scotches. Rarer labels—especially the Lowland and Island malts—are not generally available in large discount liquor sections. Look for them on the shelves of gourmet specialty shops or enjoy them as a special treat during a trip to Europe.

Bell's—A top-selling brand on the British market, Bell's is also becoming appreciated in the United States and Canada. It's slightly sweet in flavor and suitable for mixing.

Black & White—Created by the dynamic James Buchanan in the early 20th century, this brand is now owned by DCL. Its symbol is a pair of black-and-white terrier dogs. This full-flavored blend was originally sold under the name "House of Commons" after Buchanan had secured a contract to supply Scotch to members of the British Parliament.

Dewar's White Label;
Grand Macnish;
J & B Rare;
Grant's Scotch Whisky;
Johnnie Walker Red Label.

Cutty Sark—This pale, mild Scotch was named after a famous clipper ship of the 19th century that crossed the Atlantic in record time. It's produced with North American tastes in mind by Berry Brothers & Rudd.

Dewar's White Label—Like Black & White, this brand was established by an enterprising man about 100 years ago. Tommy Dewar's genius for publicity included some early electric billboards in London showing a Highlander in full kilt downing endless shots of Dewar's. Today it's a top-selling Scotch. Drinkers especially enjoy its fresh, clean taste on the rocks.

The Famous Grouse—A full-flavored, mature blend that has gained popularity in the United States over recent years.

Grant's Standfast—This Scotch is distilled by the company that also owns the Glenfiddich Distillery. A fair proportion of Glenfiddich Malt enriches the blend, producing a well-balanced taste.

Haig—Like several other distilleries, this one claims to have been the first to introduce grain whisky into their blend. The family firm dates back to the 17th century and was an early pioneer of the continuous still. In 1877, the Haigs were founding members of DCL. Haig is a rich, malty blend.

J&B Rare—The name comes from the London wine merchants Justerini & Brooks. However, this brand is now owned by International Distillers & Vintners Ltd., not to be confused with DCL. Popular in America, it has a pleasant and light taste that suits the modern drinker.

Whyte & Mackay's 21 Years Old;
VAT 69 Reserve;
Johnnie Walker Black Label;
Grant's Royal 12 Years Old;
Ballantine's 30-year-old.

Johnnie Walker Red Label—This is one of the world's best-known Scotch blends. It is medium-flavored in style and perfect for sipping straight.

Long John—This brand is especially popular in Britain. It is named for its maker, Long John MacDonald, who was described by those who knew him as a "a happy-hearted Hercules." It includes malt Scotch from the company's Tormore distillery.

Teacher's Highland Cream—Generally rated as one of the finest of the popular brands, second only to more expensive Scotches. Its malty flavor leaves a clean "finish" on your palate.

Usher's Green Stripe—This medium-priced Scotch differs from the more expensive blends insofar as it is sold at 80 proof instead of 86 proof. It is bottled in the United States, not Scotland. Other well-known Scotches in this category are Passport, House of Stuart and King George. If you plan to mix your Scotch, you may want to consider these less-expensive brands.

VAT 69—This brand was created when William Sanderson made 100 different blends and asked tasters to choose their favorite. Obviously, they liked the 69th one best. The blend has a mature style and earthy taste. Like Usher's, it is bottled in the United States.

White Horse—A popular blend originated by the Mackie family, one of the Scotch whisky barons of the early

years. It's traditionally based on Lagavulin malt from the Isle of Islay, which gives it a peaty flavor.

Whyte & Mackay—The company was founded in 1844 by James Whyte and Charles Mackay in Glasgow. Their own brand was based on 35 Highland malt whiskies, with selected grain whiskies added. Today the drink is known as Whyte & Mackay's Special Scotch. The blend is aged after malt and grain have been mixed, a relatively unusual extra process that adds smoothness.

DELUXE SCOTCH BLENDS

The blender's art is shown at its best in these special Scotches, mixed from the finer vats available to each particular distiller. Some, like Johnnie Walker Black Label, carry names that are similar to a lower-priced, popular brand. Others, like Chivas Regal, are sold only as deluxe products.

Each deluxe blend normally contains a higher proportion of malt than a popular Scotch. It is also matured for a longer period. Many are higher in strength—about 86 proof or more. These premium whiskies are sometimes known as *liqueur Scotches*, but don't confuse them with sweetened cordials or liqueurs.

It's common to see a reference to the age of the Scotch on the labels of these bottles. This, by law, should mean that this is the age of the *youngest* whisky in the blend, not just an average age of all the components. Therefore, a 12-year-old Scotch actually contains older ingredients.

From a gift-giver's point of view, these premium Scotches are attractively presented in special boxes. The bottles have elaborate labels and distinctive shapes. Their appeal tends to be greatest at Christmas.

Johnnie Walker Black Label is a best-seller worldwide. Another familiar name is Chivas Regal. This distillery is owned by the giant Seagram Corporation, famous for its association with Canadian whiskies. Another important Canadian Scotch distiller is Hiram Walker. It produces Ballantine Scotch, with a choice of deluxe bottlings of different ages.

Most whisky companies known for their ordinary blended Scotches make deluxe versions too, like VAT 69 and Grants. Special Haig Scotch in the rounded dimple bottle is well liked, as are Antiquary, Buchanan's and Old Parr.

The finer Scotch blends should be served straight—never mixed—so their subtle flavors can be fully appreciated. A little ice and water is OK, however. Otherwise, serve them straight as very special after-dinner drinks.

21

SCOTCH MALT WHISKY

Several important factors make malt whisky a truly unique drink. Many have tried to imitate the style without success. In fact, the Japanese have gone to great expense in building distilleries exactly like those in Scotland, complete with shining copper pot stills. Yet the end result, while drinkable and even impressive, does not completely resemble Scotch malt whisky. In frustration, some Japanese distillers have begun to import casks of Scottish-made malt whiskies to add to their own blends.

What are the special qualities of a Scottish-distilled malt? Experts say that true malt whisky has a unique smoky, or peaty quality. This is derived in part from the peat used to dry the malted barley. Other factors are the fresh waters of Highland Springs and the cold, moist Scottish climate.

At least 120 malt distilleries are scattered throughout Scotland, but the greatest concentration is found on the banks of the River Spey in the Highlands. The products of most of these go directly to one of the big blending companies to be used in their famous-brand Scotches. The remainder is bottled as single malts, meaning that they are the *unblended* products of a single distillery.

Somewhere between the blended Scotches and single-malt Scotches comes a relatively new invention—the blended malt. These are unblended malts from several different distilleries that have been mixed to produce a unique product. Many blended malts are now available, including Dewar's 12-year-old, Glencoe, and Strathspey. To avoid confusion with true blends, which include both grain and malt whiskies, blended malts are often called *vatted malts*. If you're new to the taste of malt Scotch, one of these could be a good and relatively inexpensive introduction.

The major areas for production of malt whisky are the Highlands, Lowlands and the Islands of Scotland. Highland malts are the great majority and considered the finest of the malt world. Malts from the islands—Islay, Skye and Jura—have a reputation for their strong and distinctive flavors. If you take to the peatiness of a Scotch like Laphroaig, you may become a convert to this style.

HIGHLAND MALTS

The green Scottish moors are dotted with distilleries, some of them dating back to the time of Macbeth.

The Balvenie—A top-quality malt from Dufftown, in the heart of the Scotch-making country. Visitors to this distillery see a rare sight—traditional "maltings" with workers laboriously preparing the barley by hand. Most malted barley now comes from giant central suppliers. Many times the barley has been imported from California, Canada, India or Africa.

Cardhu—A 12-year-old single malt that is made by the Johnnie Walker company on Speyside. In Celtic, the name means *black rock*. Like most Highland malts, it's light in body and not too smoky.

Dufftown Glenlivet—The name *Glenlivet* has been added to this Scotch to give additional prestige. The original Glenlivet—known today as *The Glenlivit*—was the first, and some still consider the finest, of all Highland malts.

Glendronach—Whisky with a fairly sharp flavor. The distillery is owned by William Teacher & Sons. Like many other Highland distilleries, it's built by the waters of a special stream.

Glenfarclas—A wide range of proof strengths and ages is marketed by this distillery. The label may indicate that the Scotch inside is from 8 to 25 years old. Older Scotches cost more, although experts generally agree that there is no marked improvement in a Scotch after 15 years in cask. This family-owned distillery is rated among the most distinguished in the field of single malts.

Glenfiddich—Another family-owned business, William Grant, controls this famous name. It also owns Balvenie and some blended styles. The dynamism of this family group has been remarkable since the first Scotch flowed from the Glenfiddich stills on Christmas Day 1887. The reputation of this malt has been among the best ever since. The name means "Valley of the Deer," and the stag is a symbol of this brand. It has delicate peatiness and a lingering, slightly sweet flavor.

Glen Grant—Founded in 1840, this brand is associated with The Glenlivet. It is an assertive style of malt that some prefer to serve with a little water.

The Glenlivet—It's a famous Scotch that comes from Scotland's first legal distillery, registered by a far-seeing farmer called George Smith in 1823. At this period illicit distilling was rife. Smith's move to become legal incurred the wrath of his associates. But his gamble paid off—his whisky began to be known far and wide. Today The Glenlivet is owned by the giant Seagram Corporation. To many, it's synonymous with malt Scotch, and is widely available. In flavor it is rather fruity and well balanced.

Glenmorangie—A very popular malt worldwide, due to its distinctive pale color and lightness of flavor. It is made with water from the Springs of Tarlogie, said to give it a slight mineral taste.

The MaCallan—High quality and small production make this an expensive brand, appreciated by the true malt enthusiast. It is rich and smooth to the taste.

Tomatin—A fine malt from the Highlands' largest malt distillery, built at the turn of the century. It has only recently begun exporting its dry, fruity-flavored Scotch to North America.

LOWLAND MALTS

In the Lowlands, malt distillers are extremely proud of their one-of-kind Scotches.

Auchentoshan—Much of the production from this distillery, 10 miles north of Glasgow, goes into the big city for blending. But some is sold as a single malt that contrasts markedly with the classic Highland style. It is light, soft and very smooth on the palate.

Rosebank—From a distillery built in 1824 on the banks of an old canal. Like most lowland malts, it is well-balanced, dry and not as smoky as the Highland whiskies.

ISLAND AND CAMPBELTOWN MALTS

There's a special romance associated with Island malts. The distilleries are nestled in some of the most beautiful scenery in the world.

Bowmore—A fairly gentle Islay malt, it is less smoky and pungent than other famous names. In its third century of Scotch distilling, this company is situated in spectacular surroundings on the Isle of Islay.

Lagavulin—This distillery is owned by the makers of White Horse blended Scotch, who boast that the addition of this Islay malt gives their blend a classic "peat reek" of smoke and heather, along with a powerful flavor.

Laphroaig—A malt with a considerable following in North America. Its distinctive flavor, however, may not suit every taste. The current style is now slightly mellower in flavor than the old. The distillery is owned by the makers of Long John.

Talisker—Here is a Scotch Malt from the beautiful Isle of Skye. Said to have a flavor of seaweed, it is renowned for its powerful aftertaste. It is generally available in the United States.

HOW TO SERVE MALTS

The purist would never allow anything to dilute his malt, except perhaps a few drops of Highland spring water. Less fanatical types may add a little ice. Always remember that the flavor of these rare whiskies is delicate and elusive. They are at their best on a cool winter evening, served after dinner as you would a fine Cognac brandy.

The Balvenie;
Bruichladdich;
Glenmorangie;
Glenfiddich.

IRISH WHISKEY

The Irish pride themselves on the ancientness of their whiskey-making tradition. Somewhere between the 5th and 10th centuries A.D. the first "water of life" was distilled on the island by monks who had learned this skill from visitors from continental Europe. The difference between the Irish spirit and its ancestors was a base of cereal grains rather than wine. This was necessary because cereals like barley grew abundantly on the Emerald Isle. Grape vines couldn't grow due to the Irish climate.

During the early years of the 17th century the Irish introduced taxes on whiskey in an attempt to curb drunkenness. Whiskey making then went underground. Thousands of illegal stills for the making of *potheen*, or pot-still liquor, were set up by enterprising Irishmen. To this day, many hidden stills are in the Irish countryside.

In 1779, a still tax was implemented in Ireland. In 10 years the number of legal distilleries dropped from well over 1000 to 246. By 1900, this number declined to about 30, centered mainly in Dublin, Belfast and Cork.

Further closures continued until 1966, when the remaining big three companies—John Jameson, John Power and the Cork Distillery Company—amalgamated to form the Irish Distillers Group, Ltd. They are now the sole remaining legal producers of Irish whiskey, with 16 different brands. Their main distillery is at Midleton in the Irish Republic. The company also controls the ancient distillery at Old Bushmills in County Antrim, Northern Ireland. This still has been in continuous operation since 1608, possibly making it Europe's oldest.

HOW IRISH WHISKEY IS MADE

Irish whiskeys may be compared with Scottish malts, because they are made in pot stills with barley as the basic ingredient. But this barley is also mixed with smaller quantities of wheat, oats and rye.

Malting—Barley is allowed to sprout on the floor of the malt house. It is then dried in kilns fired by hard-coal blazes. No smoky taste is imparted to the malt.

Fermentation—The malt is mixed with unmalted barley and other ground or crushed cereals. Then the mixture goes into a mash tun, where warm water is added. Revolving rakes stir the mash, blending the sugars from the malt into the liquid. The liquid mash, or *wort*, then goes to another vat for fermentation

Distillation—The wash is distilled three times, not twice as in Scotland. The third distillation extracts all possible alcohol from the wash.

Maturation—As a result of the triple distillation, Irish whiskey has a higher concentration of alcohol than Scotch when it goes into cask. It is often about 170 proof. Sherry, rum, brandy or bourbon casks are used for aging.

Warehouse conditions affect each whiskey's eventual strength. In a dry, warm storeroom the spirit will evaporate fairly rapidly and become stronger. But in a typically damp, cool Irish warehouse the spirit actually absorbs moisture and loses some of its alcoholic strength. Irish whiskeys must be aged at least four years.

BRANDS OF IRISH WHISKEYS

The classic Irish toast is the Celtic *Slainte!*—meaning *To your health!* Say it next time you try one of these whiskeys.

Murphy's—Blended with the American taste in mind, this whiskey has a fruity, soft flavor.

Jameson—One of the famous names in Irish whiskey, Jameson comes from a distillery that was founded in 1780.

Paddy Old Irish Whiskey; John Power & Son Irish Whiskey; Jameson Irish Whiskey; Old Bushmills Black Bush.

Its principal whiskey in the worldwide market is a blend of various pot-still whiskeys matured in charred American-oak barrels. It has a fragrant aroma and nutty flavor, typical of the Irish style. Jameson also markets other whiskeys, including Jameson Crested Ten. This blend of older pot-still whiskeys is matured in sherry casks with older whiskeys such as Jameson 12-year-old, and John Jameson Very Special Old Whiskey—their top-of-the-line label.

Paddy—The second-largest-selling whiskey in Ireland. It is blended from three whiskey types—a straight pot-still malt from the old original Midleton distillery, another whiskey made with both malted and unmalted barley and a grain whiskey. It has a woody flavor and is quite sharp in style.

Power's Gold Label—In Ireland, it is said that you can tell a whiskey-drinker's religion by his choice of brand—Power's is for Catholics and Jameson's for Protestants. This particular blend includes both pot-still and grain whiskeys. It has a bright golden color and a very smooth finish, set off by a slight sweetness.

Old Bushmills—Chiefly a single malt from the pot still, this whiskey has very little grain whiskey added for smoothness. It is relatively heavy in style with some sweetness in taste. The same company also markets a premium brand called Old Bushmills Black Bush. It is dry in style and warming in flavor.

HOW TO SERVE IRISH WHISKEY

You can drink Irish whiskey straight, on ice or mixed. It's great all three ways. Enjoy it on St. Patrick's day in a bright-green Irish cocktail. Mix one jigger of Irish whiskey with three dashes of crème de menthe and six dashes of green Chartreuse. Shake with ice and strain into a chilled cocktail glass.

Try delicious Irish coffee, a bracing hot beverage. Pour a jigger of Irish whiskey into a cup of freshly made strong black coffee, add sugar to taste, then stir. Carefully add a layer of cold, heavy cream, or spoon on a dollop of whipped cream. Neither type of cream should be stirred into the coffee.

25

CANADIAN WHISKY

As with Scotland's preference, this is whiskey without the *e*. The reason is that Scottish immigrants played a major part in the origins of Canadian whisky.

During the 18th century, Scotland was a poor country, with few jobs, making Canada an attractive alternative. On arrival in the New World, those with a knowledge of distillation found grain plentiful and cheap. Barley, however, was not commonly cultivated. After some trial and error, Scotsmen managed to reduce the quantities of barley malt required in their whisky formulas. To make up the difference, they added corn, wheat and rye to the mash. Canadian whisky is also popularly known as *rye*, although the exact proportions of rye to other grains have never been laid down by law.

The oldest distillery operating in Canada was founded in 1832 in the town of York, today called Toronto. The partners in this venture were named Gooderham and Worts. Their Canadian business did so well that it even began to export casks of its Old Rye whisky back to Britain.

Several notable family firms began at this time—firms which have since become giant international corporations. The largest of them all is the Seagram Company, founded by Joseph E. Seagram in 1857.

Later a distillery was set up at Beaupré, on the shores of the St. Lawrence River below Quebec. The enterprise rapidly expanded, halted only by Prohibition in America. When Prohibition ended, the firm was in the hands of Samuel Bronfman, who built up the company to its present enormous success.

Another notable figure in the history of Canadian whisky was Hiram Walker, whose company today runs second to Seagram in sales. Walker's Canadian Club brand is known throughout the world.

HOW CANADIAN WHISKIES ARE MADE

Canada possesses rich natural resources. It has a good portion of the world's fresh water supplies, and vast amounts of grain are grown in the prairie states. Because distillers use the continuous (patent) still, large amounts of Canadian whisky are made—enough for both domestic and export sale.

Preparing The Mash—It is usually made of large amounts of corn, with some rye and barley. Although many drinkers refer to Canadian whisky as *rye*, government regulations simply state that "Canadian rye whisky shall be whisky distilled in Canada, and shall possess the aroma, taste and character generally attributable to Canadian whisky." The whisky must be made from cereal grains only, but the proportions of each grain are up to the individual distiller.

The usual ratio is about seven parts corn to one part rye. The cereals are mashed with warm water to encourage the release of their natural sugars.

Fermentation—Cereal mash is transferred to a fermentation vat, where yeasts are introduced to start fermentation. This usually takes from three to five days.

Distillation—Fermented mash goes for distillation in a continuous still. After one distillation, the spirit is known as *high wine*. Most distillers then cut this strong spirit with pure water and rectify it to get a neutral spirit. Unlike Scotch distillers, Canadians do not seek to retain the *congeners*—powerful flavoring ingredients derived from the raw materials used to make the whisky.

Maturation—The neutral spirit passes into old, charred bourbon barrels or into new white-oak casks for aging. The minimum maturing time by law is three years before blending or sale. The Canadian government does not regulate aging and blending procedures as strictly as the governments of other whisky-making countries. Any loss of volume by evaporation during aging may be made up with new spirit. The result is light-tasting, pale-colored whisky.

Blending—About 10% pure rye whisky is usually added to give extra flavor. A little caramel may also be put in for color. The whisky may then be sold or returned to the barrel for further maturation, as is the case with fine blends. Most Canadian whiskies are sold at 80 U.S. proof, but premium brands are bottled at a powerful 86.8 proof. All Canadian whiskies are blends—U.S. regulations do not allow them to be labeled as *straights*.

BRANDS OF CANADIAN WHISKIES

During Prohibition, millions of bottles of Canadian whiskey were smuggled into the United States. Afterward,

drinkers retained brand loyalty.

Seagram's V.O.—A premium blend made from whiskies from Seagram's six Canadian distilleries. A bottle of this fine spirit may include up to 120 different whisky batches. *V.O.* stands for *very old*.

Calvert Distillers—The Seagram company owns this distillery and produces a deluxe blend called Calvert Masterpiece. It also distills Canadian Lord Calvert, a blend that is sent to the U.S for bottling to save on import taxes. Other subsidiary companies of the Seagram organization are Crown Royal, Antique, Gold Stripe and Royal Charter. All make whiskies that have a mellow flavor and light body.

Canadian Club—A pleasant whisky, it's the major label of the Hiram Walker Company. In addition, Hiram Walker makes other brands, including Carleton Tower, Imperial and Gold Crest. Their subsidiary company, called Barclay's, markets various brands, including Barclay Square.

Black Velvet—This smooth-tasting whisky is a product of Gilbey's Canada and is sold under the banner of the Heublein corporation. It is usually among the top-selling spirits in North America. Other brands from Gilbey's include Number Eight, Triple Crown and Colony House.

Windsor Supreme—Another popular brand in North America sold by National Distillers. Windsor Supreme has a delicate taste.

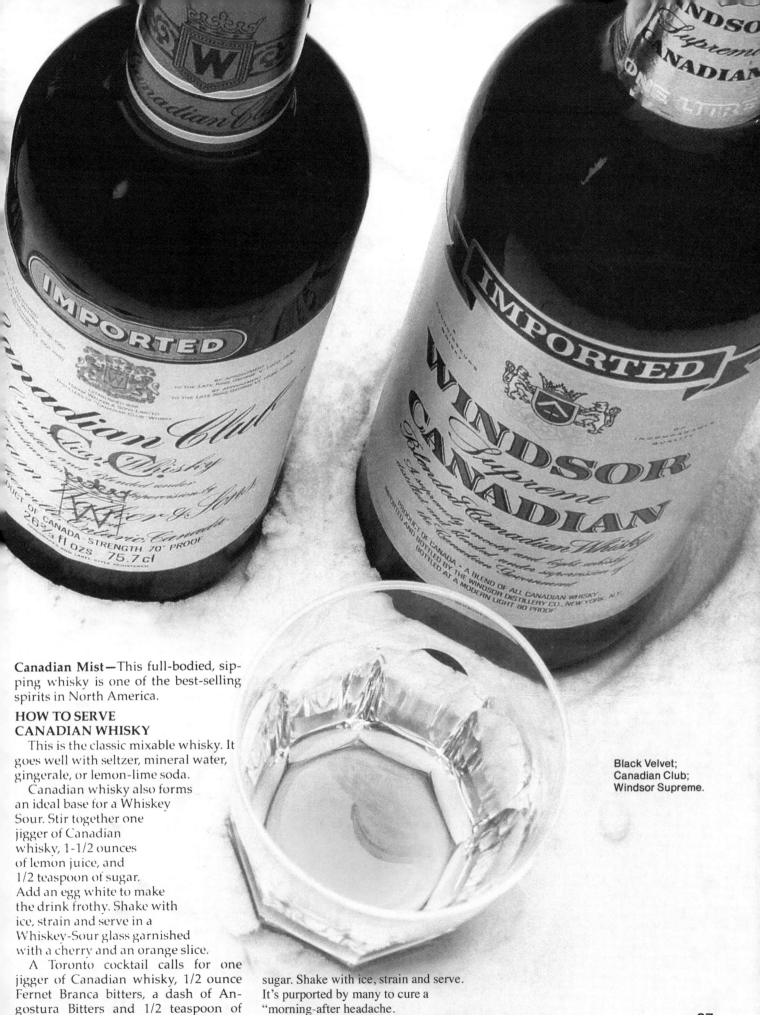

Canadian Mist—This full-bodied, sipping whisky is one of the best-selling spirits in North America.

HOW TO SERVE CANADIAN WHISKY

This is the classic mixable whisky. It goes well with seltzer, mineral water, gingerale, or lemon-lime soda.

Canadian whisky also forms an ideal base for a Whiskey Sour. Stir together one jigger of Canadian whisky, 1-1/2 ounces of lemon juice, and 1/2 teaspoon of sugar. Add an egg white to make the drink frothy. Shake with ice, strain and serve in a Whiskey-Sour glass garnished with a cherry and an orange slice.

A Toronto cocktail calls for one jigger of Canadian whisky, 1/2 ounce Fernet Branca bitters, a dash of Angostura Bitters and 1/2 teaspoon of sugar. Shake with ice, strain and serve. It's purported by many to cure a "morning-after headache.

Black Velvet;
Canadian Club;
Windsor Supreme.

27

SOUTHEASTERN UNITED STATES

AMERICAN WHISKEY

The history of the United States is closely associated with that of many other countries. Immigrants from all over Europe have flocked to its shores for centuries. Therefore, it's hardly surprising that they brought with them knowledge of distilling and a desire to make a good version of what they had enjoyed drinking back home.

A BRIEF HISTORY

The Dutch established some of the first legal stills in the United States. However, these pioneers were likely to have concocted an American version of their Genever gin, rather than anything associated with whiskey.

Distilled beverages of all kinds were made during the 17th century. They included rum made from West Indian molasses, applejack from wild apples, and *peray* from pears.

Water supplies of the Colonial period were not reliably clean, and spirit of some kind helped to purify water for everyday drinking. Alcoholic spirits were so important to community health that local ordinances were passed declaring the necessity of a supply of distilled spirit to "maintain the morale of the farmworker."

The first pot stills making something like whiskey are said to have been established in Pennsylvania during the early 18th century. Irish immigrants flooded to the New World during the depression in the textile industry in 1716-17. Together with Scottish settlers, they became the first serious whiskey makers.

Soon homemade spirits, along with furs and guns, became a major means of exchange on the frontier. Every moderately successful farmer had his own home still, with which he distilled his excess grain. George Washington had his own distillery at Mount Vernon, managed for him by a Scotsman named James Anderson.

When the British passed an act restricting the importation of molasses to the Colonies in 1733, rum distillers were forced to rely on smuggled goods. Locally grown grains became the substitute for molasses, and whiskey-type spirits became popular. Congress voted supplies of rye as a necessity for the beleaguered Yankee army.

After the Revolution, many early settlers moved inland toward western Pennsylvania, Maryland, Kentucky and Virginia. Bumper crops of rye and corn were soon commonplace in these states. Whiskey making was economically wise for the farmer. A horse could carry two hogsheads of whiskey that brought six times the value of two sacks of grain—and the demand for strong spirits in the East was growing.

In 1791 the war-impoverished new government levied a tax of 54¢ per gallon on the capacity of every still and an extra 7¢ on each gallon of actual whiskey produced. Revenue officers were assigned to collect this tax in cash. This infuriated the fiercely independent distillers.

Unfortunate tax collectors were tarred and feathered. People rioted. In 1794, President Washington finally had to send militia to quell the uprisings of the so-called Whiskey Rebellion. By this time, some disgruntled distillers had already packed up and moved westward to the wilds of Kentucky, where for awhile they evaded the clutches of the tax man. But in the end, as in earlier Scotland, the pioneer whiskey makers had to bow to government pressure and register their stills.

Kentucky proved a lucky choice for the immigrants. The limestone-filtered springs there were as pure as those of Scotland.

The first bourbon whiskey is said to have been made by the Reverend Elijah Craig in 1789. He used a mash with a large proportion of corn, but probably didn't actually age his spirits in charred-oak bourbon barrels. Before the Civil War, Kentucky distillers almost always sold their new whiskeys immediately. Aging, if any, was done by the buyer.

Despite this fact, one of the many legends about the origin of charred-barrel aging involves Elijah Craig. It seems that he was called away just as he was heating the staves to make a cask. On his return, the staves were heavily charred. To his surprise, the whiskey aged in the charred barrel had the smoothest taste. The new drink was named *bourbon*, after the county in which it was invented.

HOW AMERICAN WHISKEYS ARE MADE

There are three major styles of American whiskeys—straights, blends and light whiskeys. The largest share of the market is taken by blends, which are made up of a number of straight whiskeys.

There are six types of straight whiskeys. A mash formula of 51% or more corn makes straight bourbon, but if the corn runs to 80% or more, it becomes straight corn whiskey. Mashes with 51% or more rye, wheat, barley malt or rye malt make straight whiskeys named accordingly. Bourbon and rye are commonly sold in the straight form, but the others are used almost exclusively for blending.

Preparing The Mash—Various cooked and mashed cereals are mixed with water. A small amount of barley malt is added to aid the breakdown of starches. The mash is continually mixed with large blades to prevent it from solidifying.

Fermentation—The cereal mixture, or wort, is fermented by the action of various yeasts. If the yeast used is entirely new and fresh, the yeasting process is called *sweet mash*. *Sour mash*, on the other hand, is produced by adding working yeast from a previous fermentation to the fresh yeast. The wash from a sour-mash vat has a slightly acid taste, but the whiskey it produces is not bitter or unpleasant. Most American bourbons are made with the sour-mash process.

Distillation—All American whiskeys these days are made with the continuous still. The early pioneers used the pot still. Later when the continuous still came into general use, it was found to be ideal for making America's smooth and not-too-pungent whiskeys.

From the continuous still comes a

Mount Vernon, Virginia in 1859. Photo by William England.

neutral spirit with a high alcoholic content. Unlike many Scotches, American whiskeys are also cut with pure water at distillation rather than after maturation. Certain minimum and maximum strengths are dictated by law. For instance, bourbon must be aged at not more than 125 proof and bottled at not less than 80 proof.

Maturation—This is where you'll find the greatest differences between the various American whiskeys. Bourbon and rye whiskeys are stored in new charred-oak barrels. Light whiskeys, on the other hand, are never aged in charred oak.

The resulting flavors are much different, with bourbon and rye whiskeys having an interesting full-bodied taste. Most American whiskeys are aged under warm, dry conditions. Their proof strength increases due to water evaporation.

AMERICAN WHISKEY LABELS & BRANDS

Because the U.S. whiskey scene is fairly complex, it's worthwhile to consider a few of the words and phrases you'll see on labels.

BLENDED WHISKEY

This is the most popular American style, and usually the least expensive. By law, blends must contain at least 20% by volume 100 proof straight whiskey. If a blend contains at least 51% of a certain straight whiskey, it may be called *blended bourbon, corn whiskey* or *rye,* according to the predominant grain.

The list of American blends is headed by Seagram's 7 Crown, the top-selling whiskey in the world. Other names under the Seagram corporate umbrella include Four Roses, Antique, Wilson, Calvert, Paul Jones, Kessler and Carstairs. The reason for 7 Crown's great popularity is probably its clean, robust taste.

The popularity of blended whiskeys varies regionally with relatively few names known on a nationwide or international basis. Most major spirit companies market their own brands. Even mass-bottled blends sold under private label can make fine mixing whiskeys.

STRAIGHT WHISKEY

By U.S. federal regulations, a straight whiskey has been distilled off at not more than 160 proof, aged in new charred-oak barrels for at least 24 months and reduced at the time of bottling to 80 to 110 proof. Although the mash is a blend of cereals containing at least 51% of a single grain, a straight whiskey is not blended with other whiskeys before aging or bottling. Only water may be added.

BLENDED AND STRAIGHT WHISKEY

This is an unusual style. It is a blend of several straight whiskeys from one or several distilleries.

BOTTLED IN BOND

Many people mistakenly believe that this term on a label is a guarantee of quality. Actually, it refers only to an Internal Revenue tax. Bottled-in-bond whiskeys have been aged in specially supervised warehouses where no tax has to be paid until the spirit is bottled. The whiskey must be at least four years old, straight and bottled at 100 proof.

Left side: Early Times;
Old Crow; Antique;
Seagram's 7 Crown.
Right side: Ancient Age;
Old Grand-Dad; Wild Turkey;
Walker's Deluxe Bourbon; Jim Beam.

BOURBON WHISKEY

This is a top-selling type of whiskey. It must contain at least 51% corn in the mash to be labeled *straight*. Usually, the mash contains about 70% corn.

Bourbon must be aged in new charred-oak casks for at least two years. Quality bourbons are generally aged for at least four years. Only whiskey made in the United States can be called *bourbon*, and the best bourbons are made in Kentucky. To be called *Kentucky bourbon*, they have to spend at least one year aging in Kentucky.

Both straight and blended bourbons make palate-pleasing drinks. The straights are generally fuller in body and flavor than the blends. Many people in the Northeastern states mistakenly refer to blended bourbon as *rye*. In fact, true rye is much stronger in flavor than ordinary bourbon blends.

Like premium Scotches, premium bourbons are aged longer and sold at least 86 proof. Many are bottled in bond. Around the holidays, you can usually find them in elegant gift-boxes.

Wild Turkey is a Kentucky straight bourbon aged for at least eight years and bottled at 101 proof. Some other premium brands include Benchmark, Eagle Rare, I. W. Harper, Old Fitzgerald, Old Forester, Old Grand-Dad, Walker's Deluxe Bourbon and Weller's Special Reserve. Among these, Old Forester has the historical distinction of being the first bourbon to be sold in a bottle. Prior to 1872, all whiskey was poured directly from the cask into the customer's own container.

All premium bourbons have subtle aroma, flavor and body. They should always be served alone—either straight or on ice. For making cocktails and long drinks, a popular, less expensive bourbon is a better buy.

Another popular bourbon, Old Crow, was founded by the Scotsman Dr. James Crow. He built his distillery in 1835 and used his scientific knowledge to improve quality standards for the benefit of the whole whiskey industry.

Other popular 80-proof bourbons are Early Times, Sunnybrook and Ten High. Ancient Age is sold at 86 proof, but in mellowness and flavor it remains in the popular category. Don't be afraid to experiment with brands —even the mass-bottled blends sold under private labels can be good in cocktails.

LIGHT WHISKEY

This was first made in 1972 with the idea of competing as a cocktail mixer with popular white spirits like vodka and white rum. Because it is distilled at a very high proof, it loses most of its flavor in the still. The result is a pale whiskey with an almost grain-neutral flavor.

RYE WHISKEY

Like bourbon, this may be bottled as *straight rye*, indicating that it is the unblended product of one distillery. To be labeled *straight rye*, the spirit must contain at least 51% rye grain in the mash. *Blended straight rye* is a mix of several straights from various distilleries. *Blended rye* is a mix of various whiskeys from one or more distilleries.

SOUR MASH

The name means that the whiskey has been made by the sour-mash yeasting process. Some bourbons made from sour mash do not say so on the label. This is probably because their advertising agencies think the word *sour* will turn away buyers.

TENNESSEE WHISKEY

This is a straight whiskey of 90 proof. It's filtered through finely ground sugar-maple charcoal to give a smooth flavor. Then it's aged in charred-oak barrels for four or more years.

Tennessee whiskey was pioneered in part by Jack Daniel. He perfected the unique way in which his whiskey is made. It involves slow filtration through charcoal in 12-foot-high vats.

Today, Jack Daniel's whiskey is considered by many to be the finest available. It's made at Lynchburg in one of the oldest U.S. distilleries. The green-label type is at least four years old; the black-label type is at least five years old. The premium black label is the one you'll see most often outside the South.

Two other venerable Tennessee whiskeys are George A. Dickel and Ezra Brooks. Like Jack Daniel's, these spirits offer a special flavor that can't be duplicated outside the state of Tennessee.

HOW TO SERVE AMERICAN WHISKEY

There are dozens of cocktails based on American whiskeys, especially on blended bourbons. The famous drink of the Old South is the Mint Julep. To make one, you need a teaspoon of sugar, four sprigs of spearmint and one jigger of quality bourbon. Mash the mint and sugar together in an Old-Fashioned glass or silver mug, then gently add the bourbon. Fill the glass with shaved ice and stir until it is frosted. Garnish with another sprig of fresh mint.

Another famous bourbon-based drink is the Manhattan. Take one jigger of bourbon or rye, plus 1/2 ounce of sweet or dry vermouth. Add a drop of Angostura Bitters and stir well with ice cubes. Strain into a stemmed cocktail glass and garnish with a cherry.

For an Old Fashioned, mix a teaspoonful of sugar with a dash of Angostura Bitters in an Old-Fashioned glass. Stir in the whiskey, add ice cubes and garnish with a cherry and an orange slice.

The Highball, a term now used to describe any long cocktail, was once a specific bourbon-based drink. Pour one jigger of Bourbon over ice, then add gingerale to taste. This drink is commonly known today as a *Seven & Seven*, because it's frequently made with Seagram's 7 blend and the soda 7-Up.

OTHER WHISKEYS

Whiskey-type spirits are also produced in Holland, Germany, Denmark, Spain and Britain. In general, they're not available in America and are are inferior to the premium products of Scotland, Ireland, Canada and America. Exceptions to this are the distinctive whiskeys of Australia, New Zealand and Japan, which deserve special consideration.

JAPANESE WHISKEYS

Since the late 1940s, Japan has become a major distilling nation, notably of whiskey. This achievement is largely due to the efforts of one company—Suntory.

Today whiskey has replaced the traditional sake as the major Japanese spirit. Suntory sells more than 30 million cases a year in Japan.

Their premium whiskeys have a relatively high proportion of Scotch malt in the blend. This is exported to Japan in the cask. The top Suntory whiskey is simply called The Whisky—only 6,000 bottles are made

each year. Other premium labels include Imperial, Excellence, Royal and Special Reserve. In America, Imperial is known as Signature.

Other Japanese distilleries are Nikka, with brands including G & G, Super Nikka and Black Nikka.

AUSTRALIAN AND NEW ZEALAND WHISKEYS

During the Second World War, supplies of Scotch whisky to Australia were stopped, so domestic whiskey came into its own. The process is a very close imitation of that used in Scotland to make the popular blended styles. The flavor tends to be rather softer than Scotch, though similar.

Brands include Bond 7, made by Gil-bey's, which also makes Gilt Edge. Another fine brand is Corio, made by United Distillers. The area of production is around Melbourne, where the water supply is said to be the purest, and the barley and corn are of superior quality.

The history of commercial whiskey making in nearby New Zealand goes back only to 1969, when the Wilson Distillers Company of Dunedin began making their blended styles. Well-known brands are 45 South and Wilson's Matured Blend. They are made in a manner similar to Scotch, but aged in American bourbon casks. They are sweeter and fuller bodied than Australian whiskeys.

Vodka

Since the late 1940s, vodka has been a great success worldwide. It's most popular as a versatile cocktail and highball spirit. Yet when this drink originated in Russia long ago, it was never mixed. It was consumed cold and straight, tossed back in one fiery gulp.

ORIGINS AND HISTORY

The name of this spirit derives from the Russian phrase *zhiznennia voda*, meaning *water of life*. The word *vodka* is an affectionate nickname meaning *little water*.

There's some evidence that a strong, colorless spirit similar to vodka was made in Persia in the 11th century. Russians, however, maintain that vodka was invented in their country during the 1300s at the fort of Viataka. Most historians concede that the Russians did originate their national drink, but do not agree on its date of origin.

The secret of distilling neutral spirits from starchy substances soon spread from Russia to neighboring Finland. It also crept into Poland, where at first it was used only by a small number of monks, apothecaries and noble families. By the 16th century, however, many more Poles knew how to make vodka. In 1546, King Jan Olbrecht passed a law allowing every citizen to make and sell spirits. Nearly every family prepared its own vodkas, often flavoring them with fruits and herbs.

In 1780, the Russian Czar hired a chemist named Theodore Lowitz to find a way to make the nation's favorite spirit more hygenic. Lowitz invented the technique of purifying vodka by filtering it through charcoal. About 40 years later, an enterprising Moscow family—Smirnoff—established a firm with a name that has since become synonymous with vodka.

Originally just one small vodka maker among many others, the Smirnoff company made its fortune when Czar Alexander III awarded it a royal monopoly to supply vodka and vodka-based liqueurs to the Imperial Court.

This coup was achieved by a clever attention-getting ploy. Petya Smirnoff, then head of the firm, had an elaborate drinking pavilion built at a large fair. For waiters, he hired entertainers to dress as bears. They were assisted at the bar by a real bear who was trained to taste and serve vodka from a tray. The animal offered a frosty glass of Smirnoff vodka to the Czar, who approved with hearty amusement. This approval eventually brought enormous wealth to the Smirnoff family, until social and political disruption early in the 20th century slowed vodka production.

On the heels of World War I came the Russian Revolution, which virtually wiped out the Smirnoff family. Vladimir Smirnoff and his wife Tatiana escaped to Paris. There, Vladimir made contact with Rudolf Kunett, a Russian-born American, whose family had supplied the Smirnoffs with grain in Imperial times.

In 1934, Kunett established a small vodka distillery in Connecticut, making Smirnoff-type vodka from the formula his friend had smuggled out of Russia. Eventually, he sold the rights to Smirnoff vodka to John G. Martin, chairman of Heublein, a liquor firm based in Connecticut. This company continues to make and sell Smirnoff.

Above: Private house of the Smirnoff family next to the Iron Bride in Moscow, 1980.

Left: Portrait of Piotr Arsenovich Smirnoff, grandson of the founder of the company.

Below: The Smirnoff factories in Moscow ca. 1900.

HOW VODKA IS MADE

Vodka can be manufactured from anything that contains starch or sugar —including potatoes, molasses, corn and grapes. All of these ingredients have been used commercially, and potatoes are still sometimes used in Poland and Russia. However, the tasteless, neutral style typified by world-popular Smirnoff is principally made with corn.

Preparing The Mash—The corn is pressure-cooked and ground. In Europe, a special cone-shaped cooker is used for potatoes. The mash is cooled and mixed with water. Malts or special enzymes are added to convert the starch to sugar.

Fermentation—Yeast is added, and the wort ferments, much as in whiskey making.

Distillation—The wash goes into a continuous still, where it is distilled to a very high proof to extract all flavoring elements. Vodkas come out of the still at about 190 proof.

Purification—Continuous stills have two columns—one for distillation and one for rectification. Stills for neutral spirits have at least one additional column, where the distilled alcohol is further purified. High-quality vodkas are also filtered through tanks containing charcoal.

Bottling—The purified neutral spirit is diluted with water to decrease its alcoholic strength. No aging is required, so vodka can be bottled the same day it's made.

Vodka's popularity has grown since the late 1940s. At first it was enjoyed in the Russian style—gulped cold from tiny glasses.

Then one day the proprietor of a well-known tavern in Los Angeles found himself with a huge overstock of Schweppe's gingerale. In desperation he tried mixing it with every spirit he had behind the bar, but nothing worked until he tried a jigger of neutral-tasting vodka. He added the juice of half a lime, garnished it with the rind and triumphantly dubbed it the *Moscow Mule*. It was the first of a string of sensationally successful cocktails that induced many distilleries to make vodka.

Today about 200 brands of vodka are available. They are made in the U.S. and in Poland, Finland, Russia, France, Holland and elsewhere. There is even a Kosher vodka from Israel.

WHY IT IS POPULAR

The biggest reason for vodka's popularity with modern drinkers is that it doesn't add strong flavor to a cocktail, making a drink that's often deceptively mild and "spiritless." Nor does it have any smell, implied in the famous advertising slogan, "It leaves you breathless."

Vodka also has a reputation for being the purest of spirits—the one least likely to leave you with a hangover. This last claim has some validity, because vodka contains no residual flavoring elements to be processed by your digestive system.

Despite its neutral taste and water-like appearance, the national drink of Russia is definitely a strong spirit, usually made from 80 to 100 proof. Vodkas made in other countries are sometimes stronger, ranging from 120 to 160 U.S. proof.

HOW TO SERVE VODKA

Many legends surround vodka drinking. You probably have an image of a fur-clad Russian tossing back glass after glass of the powerful drink, then smashing his tumbler into the fireplace. Actually, such toasts were usually limited to one, and the glasses were so small that they held an ounce or less. They were made to break easily after drinking a toast to the Czar. This guaranteed that the glass would not be defiled by toasting a lesser person.

Although wanton destruction of glassware has become a thing of the past, an attractive small glass with a slender stem does add to the pleasure of drinking straight vodka. The finest brands have a slight oiliness that's best appreciated in clear crystal.

Unlike straight whiskey, vodka should never be served at room temperature. Pour it from a bottle that's been well chilled in the refrigerator or freezer. To be elegant, fill a jigger with cold vodka and place it in a nest of crushed ice inside an Old-Fashioned glass. Or, try offering it to your guests on the rocks, garnished with a twist of lemon.

In Russia, straight vodka is always served with food. The classic accompaniment is caviar, but any highly seasoned hors d'oeuvre will do. The icy tang of the straight spirit cuts through the richness of the food.

Vodka Cocktails—Natually, you should serve only high-quality vodka straight. Use low-priced brands for mixed drinks. In fact, this is the way most people prefer their vodka.

There are dozens of vodka-based cocktails, and each year seems to bring a new one. The Moscow Mule, for example, has long been supplanted by the Smirnoff Mule. To make one, substitute lemon-lime soda for the original gingerale.

Almost as old is the popular Bloody Mary—a great drink for brunch. Splash a drop of Worcestershire sauce into a highball glass, then add a dash of Tabasco. Put in 1/3 jigger of lemon juice, a sprinkle of salt, a jigger of vodka and tomato juice to taste. Stir and sprinkle with freshly ground black pepper. Garnish with a lemon slice and a celery stick.

A variation is the Bullshot—cold beef consommé is substituted for tomato juice.

A Screwdriver is another refreshing vodka drink. Pour a jigger of vodka over ice, add orange juice to taste, and stir.

The Vodka Martini, sometimes called a *Vodkatini*, is an alternative to the gin-based original. Add one measure of dry vermouth to two measures of vodka. Shake with ice and serve "straight-up" or pour over ice in an Old-Fashioned glass. To make a Vodka Gibson, substitute a pickled onion for the olive or lemon garnish.

A Black Russian calls for 1 jigger of vodka and 1/2 jigger of coffee liqueur served over ice. For a White Russian, add 1/2 ounce of cream or substitute white crème de cacao for the coffee liqueur.

Vodka is perfect for adding spirit to a big bowl of fruit punch. Or, substitute it for gin in a Tonic, Collins, Fizz or other long drink.

In a Gimlet, vodka doesn't detract from the sweet-tart taste of Rose's lime juice. Use three parts vodka to one part Rose's and serve it on the rocks with a twist of fresh-cut lime peel.

Smirnoff vodka advertisements are known in the spirits industry for fresh boldness.

37

VODKAS OF THE WESTERN WORLD

These vodkas are made to appeal to general tastes. Mainly produced in North America, they have almost no flavor and no color.

One exception to this is a flavored vodka made by smaller distilleries like Chateaux. Flavored styles like these are generally associated with Eastern Europe, but even some Western countries make mint, orange, lime and cherry vodkas.

Flavored-vodka drinkers feel strongly about the brands they buy. However, brand loyalty is rare among drinkers of unflavored vodkas. Major distilleries claim that they offer a finer product made of better raw materials and filtered more thoroughly for smoothness. Yet many buyers say that even the cheapest brands fill their basic need for an 80-proof cocktail base.

It's when you want to serve vodka in a Martini or straight that the high-quality brands are important. Most premium vodkas in this group are 100 U.S. proof, which gives them a bit more impact on the taste buds.

Western vodkas reflect the romantic image we have of Czarist Russia. Many brands have Russian-sounding names, and their gilt-trimmed labels sport imposing crests. But remember that with the exception of Smirnoff, which was once Russian, all other U.S. brands are no more Russian than Tennessee Sour Mash.

Because the procedures for making vodka and gin are very similar, famous gin distillers like Gordon's and Gilbey's also make a line of vodkas. Gordon's has even patented their secret of vodka distillation. The following is a brief selection of vodkas made in the West.

Gilbey's—Popular in North America. In Britain, Gilbey's is the local distiller of Smirnoff, and does not sell the vodka under its own name.

Gordon's—From the famous makers of London Dry Gin, this is mainly available outside Britain. The label is unusual because it bears only the boar's-head emblem of the company and no Russian-style ornamentation.

Kamchatka—A best-selling brand in North America produced by the National Distillers group. It's a good, low-cost vodka.

Popov—Nothing succeeds like success, and Popov is the successful

cousin of Smirnoff—they're both made by Heublein. It sells for a little less than its famous relative and generally takes second place in market ratings.

Schenley's—This is a "house brand" from a major U.S. liquor company. Others of this type include Fleischmann's, Hiram Walker and Mr. Boston.

Smirnoff—When Vladimir Smirnoff made his escape from Russia during the Revolution, he had virtually nothing to show for the former glory of his family's company. But he did have the formula for making Smirnoff vodka. Eventually, it was made in the U.S. Now it is a product of the Heublein company, which owes much of its success to Smirnoff vodka.

Smirnoff is distilled under license in several other countries and is the indisputable world brand leader. According to Gilbey's, the British licensee, nearly five bottles of Smirnoff are sold every second, worldwide.

There are several styles of Smirnoff. The major one is the 80 U.S. proof red label. Silver label is 90 U.S. proof, and blue label is 100 U.S. proof.

Vladivar—This is Britain's number-two vodka after Smirnoff. It's rarely available in North America.

Wolfschmidt—A successful vodka made by Seagram. Other brands marketed by them include Crown Russe and Nicolai. All are good mixing vodkas. Wolfschmidt is the best to drink straight.

Zamoyski—A noble Polish name now used for a vodka distilled in Britain. The original family distillery in Poland dates back to 1601.

Wolfschmidt; Vladivar;
Smirnoff; Borzoi;
Popov; Zamoyski.

Stolichnaya;
Zubrówka;
Finlandia;
Wyborowa.

VODKAS OF RUSSIA & EASTERN EUROPE

As mentioned, high-quality vodkas are ideally consumed chilled and straight. Try it with these vodkas.

POLISH VODKAS

The major center of vodka production is Poznan, which had 49 distilleries even in the 16th century. Other important vodka-producing cities include Gdańsk and Kraków.

In Poland, pot stills are used to make high-quality vodkas. At least two, and sometimes three, distillations are necessary to get a smooth batch. As a result, some of the flavor of basic mash ingredients like sugarbeets or grain is retained in the finished spirit. This gives Polish vodkas distinctive pungency and taste.

Polish Brands—When Pablo Picasso was once asked to name the three most important new features in post-war French culture, he said, "Modern jazz, Brigitte Bardot and Polish vodka." The artist was referring to the strong, clear variety, which still has a strong following worldwide.

The best-known Polish vodkas available are Wyborowa Red Label and the stonger Blue Label. Both are made with rye.

Flavored Styles—The Poles also export a powerful vodka of more than 114 U.S. proof. This spirit has its origins in the icy Polish winters, when wine, beer and even low-proof spirits freeze. Only the strongest vodkas can be transported and remain liquid. For export, this style is usually labeled *Polish Pure Spirit* and is often used by home brewers as a base for their own liqueurs.

In the past, the Poles used such spirits to strengthen their homemade flavored vodkas. Today, however, there is a move toward commercial manufacture of these flavored styles. Many are now made under the auspices of Polmos, the state-controlled vodka distiller.

One well-known flavored style is Zubrówka. It incorporates the taste of a grass from Bialowieza National Park, where rare bison graze. The greenish vodka is said to give you the strength of the bison. In addition, it has a gentle bouquet and softness.

Starka vodka is unusual in another way. It's golden brown and aged in a cask. Traditionally, such vodka was bottled at the birth of a daughter and consumed at her wedding feast. Now it is made at high strength and flavored with Spanish Malaga wine to bring out the taste of the rye base.

Other Polish vodkas feature the tastes of berries like rowan, juniper and cherry. Some offer you the tang of green walnuts along with various herbs. All of these flavoring elements are distilled with the spirit to make a subtle-tasting drink. On the other hand, vodka liqueurs use flavorings that are introduced after distillation, along with sweetener.

RUSSIAN VODKAS

There's less emphasis on flavored vodka in Russia. Although the fabulous wealth of the Smirnoff family was in part built on sales of vodka-based liqueurs such as ashberry, these now have less importance than strong neutral vodkas.

Russian vodkas are traditionally made from grain, but they also may be distilled from any surplus farm products. Sugarbeets and potatoes are favorites.

Russian vodkas are made in three different strengths. The strongest is about 114 proof.

The best-known Russian vodkas available here include Stolichnaya and Moskovskaya. Russkaya is a lesser-known brand. These vodkas can vary in strength and quality.

Peter the Great used to sprinkle black pepper on his vodka, and today's unique Pertsovka was inspired by this habit. Dark-brown and peppery, this tonque-tingling spirit should be reserved for the brave drinker.

FINNISH VODKAS

Finlandia vodka is recognizable by its stippled glass bottle. It's generally available in liquor stores. Finlandia is a neutral-tasting vodka, not a full-flavored Eastern European style. Consequently, it's currently a popular imported vodka in North America.

41

AQUAVIT & SCHNAPPS

Although neither aquavit nor schnapps are ever labeled *vodka*, they're all basically the same spirit, made from grain or potatoes and purified until neutral.

Aquavit is popular in Denmark, which drinks about 17 million bottles of aquavit, or *akvavit*, each year. Like Eastern European vodkas, aquavit is traditionally served ice-cold in small glasses, as an accompaniment to a delicious Danish smorgasbord. It's often chased with a pale-gold beer.

HISTORY

The history of aquavit making dates back about 400 years. In Elizabethan times, Danes were known to be big drinkers, and there's reference to this in *Hamlet*. King Christian IV, noted for his drinking prowess, was also the first monarch to levy taxes on aquavit. As in Scotland during a similar period, this led to the establishment of thousands of illicit stills. It's estimated that there were about 11,000 in the early 19th century.

In 1843 the government took firm measures to force people to surrender their stills. Eventually, about 2,500 legal distilleries formed. The center of the industry was and still is Aalborg. Today, the most important producers of Danish aquavit are the Danish Distilleries of Aalborg, which produce 90% of it. Another name for aquavit in Denmark is *schnaps*, implying its similarity to Germany's favorite, *schnapps*.

WHAT'S AVAILABLE

Danes prefer their aquavit flavored, usually with caraway, cardamom or anise. The brand most commonly found outside Denmark is Aalborg Taffel Akvavit, which has been made since 1846. It's clear and has a distinctive caraway taste. The aquavit is first distilled as a high-proof neutral spirit, then re-distilled to impart the various flavorings.

This spirit is always made at 90 U.S. proof or more. A little goes a long way—bottles are relatively small. For an elegant way to serve aquavit, freeze a bottle in a block of ice.

In Sweden, Finland and Norway, aquavit is sometimes called *vodka*. Icelanders also consider aquavit their national drink. Here, however, they call it *brannvin*—which rather ominously means *Black Death*.

In Sweden, aquavit production is strictly controlled. Both flavored and unflavored styles are made. Best-known brands are Explorer and Renat, both unflavored and fiery.

Not all aquavit is clear. In 1946, Aalborg introduced a brand called Aalborg Jubilaeums, in commemoration of their first century of distilling. This good-selling aquavit is pale gold, with the flavors of dill and coriander.

A Norwegian curiosity is golden-brown Linie Aquavit, probably the only spirit whose production involves a round-trip across the ocean. It's aged in wooden casks stored in the holds of ships bound for Australia. The warm voyage lets the spirit mature rapidly and gives it a smooth taste. Upon return to Norway, the aquavit is bottled. Each label indicates the ship that carried the aquavit across the Equator.

SCHNAPPS

Unlike aquavit, German schnapps are diverse. Many Germans use the word *schnapps* to denote any strong spirit. They're not too concerned about consistency of style. In northern Germany, for example, a schnapps

called *Korn* may resemble rye whiskey, London dry gin or Genever gin.

One of the most famous brands of Korn is Doornkaat, made with malted grains and triple-distilled for a smooth taste. A secret blend of flavorings is then added, yielding a clear spirit resembling a light rye whiskey.

Furst Bismark is a well-known brand in Germany. It's made by a company that dates back to the 17th century. This spirit is matured for a year in ash vats after distillation.

In America, peppermint schnapps is common. This spirit, however, has been combined with a sweetener to become a liqueur. It has little resemblance to the dry schnapps of Germany.

HOW TO SERVE SCHNAPPS AND AQUAVIT

Although both spirits are always served straight and cold in their homelands, there's nothing to stop you from trying them on the rocks or with a little carbonated mixer. Don't be concerned if these drinks turn cloudy. Chilling causes the flavoring oils to produce a smoky effect.

If you're daring, try drinking German schnapps the Hanoverian way. Hold a tiny glass of schnapps and a larger one of beer to your lips simultaneously. Down them together for a powerful blend.

A less dramatic way to serve these spirits is to add them to strong black coffee. In Scandinavian countries, a silver coin is placed at the bottom of the cup. Coffee is poured in until the coin is no longer visible. Then aquavit is added until the coin appears again. This makes a warming finish to any meal.

Linie Aquavit;
Doornkaat Schnapps;
Aalborg Jubilaeums Akvavit;
Aalborg Akvavit.

Gin

Among the world's favorite spirits, gin is unique for two reasons. First, it is the youngest, dating back to the mid-17th century. Second, it was invented for a specific purpose by a single individual—Dr. Franciscus de la Boë (1614-1672), also known as Dr. Sylvius.

ORIGINS AND HISTORY

Dr. Sylvius was a professor of medicine at Holland's famous University of Leyden. His purpose in concocting gin was to produce an inexpensive medicine. Juniper berries have strong diuretic qualities, as does pure alcohol. By combining the two, the good doctor made a purifying tonic that many Dutchmen soon considered necessary for good health.

Of course, a clear, neutral spirit was being made in Holland before Dr. Sylvius, but it didn't have the juniper flavor. Its refreshing taste is so basic to gin-style spirits that Dr. Sylvius named his invention genièvre, the French word for juniper. The Dutch shortened it to genever, which they still call it.

The English King William III, who was born and raised in Holland, introduced genever to England. People began calling it Hollands. British troops abbreviated the word genever to gin when they first tried the drink while fighting in Holland in the 17th century.

In the 18th century, Queen Anne helped the British gin industry by raising import taxes on foreign wines and spirits and lowering taxes on British spirits. The taste of English gin suited the British people, and they soon made it England's national drink. The dry English style of gin started developing.

Gin was made by many distillers. At first, Parliament granted the right to make gin to one company, but illegal stills were common. In 1690, lawmakers repealed the monopoly, allowing any citizen to legally distill gin.

Because gin was relatively easy to produce, hundreds of people took advantage of the new law. However, relatively few actually distilled base spirit and rectified it into a high-quality London dry gin. Many merely added flavorings to cheap neutral alcohol. In fact, some disreputable people used lethal ingredients such as turpentine, making the death rate in London rise.

Vendors roamed the streets pushing carts filled with cheap gin. Seedy shops advertised, "Drunk for one penny, dead drunk for two, clean straw for nothing." The straw was to lie on while drinking and to sleep off your hangover.

Many of the urban poor of the Industrial Revolution stayed permanently intoxicated in their search for relief from the oppressed conditions in the factories. Women in particular favored gin. They bought it from pharmacists as a medicinal drink and mixed it with warm water to "soothe their nerves." Gin took on nicknames like "Ladies Delight" and "Mother's Ruin."

In The New World—Across the Atlantic in New England, gin was a commonly imported spirit. Dutch and English settlers manufactured their own, but it took third place to local rums and the new-style whiskey called bourbon.

American patriots Paul Revere and Sam Adams enjoyed cold gin together over dinner in Boston. Patrick Henry served it while tending bar at his father-in-law's establishment. George Washington surely sampled an occasional gin with water at his favorite tavern.

Before temperance was associated with religion, even the Quakers of Pennsylvania drank gin with warm water after funerals. Farther south, Virginia planters imitated English gentlemen by drinking cold gin and riding on fox hunts.

An interesting advertisement for de Kuyper's gin emphasizs its so-called medicinal qualities.

Gin Reform—The young United States never experienced the same degree of drunkenness as that of industrial London. Pioneer farmers simply didn't have time to be regularly burdened with hangovers.

In England, gin drinking began to reduce factory output. Laws were passed to control gin consumption by raising the price. As a result, beer regained some of its old popularity. To encourage beer consumption, Parliament allowed anyone who could afford an inexpensive license to sell beer. In practically every alley, dingy pubs opened overnight.

Gin distillers sought to compete with these small establishments by selling their spirits in magnificent buildings, complete with marble facades. Inside, the furnishings were opulent and the ceilings were hung with crystal chandeliers. Hundreds of these luxurious "gin palaces" appeared in England during the 19th century.

At the polished mahogany bars, gin with water was the favorite drink. Punches and cordials were also popular, served hot in gleaming mugs. Pineapple rum, French brandy and beer were served, but the drink of choice was gin.

Mixed with sugar, lemon juice and warm water, gin became a Gin Toddy. A Gin Twist substituted orange juice and rind for the lemon. The gin of this period—called *Old Tom*—was sweet, not the bone-dry spirit you enjoy in a Martini.

U.S. Popularity—Gin first became widely popular during Prohibition. Bartenders vied with one another to create recipes for gin-based cocktails with glamorous names like Blue Moon, Pink Lady and Salomé.

The subtle yet fragrant character of gin is highly adaptable to mixing. Many bartenders consider it the ideal cocktail base. Whether in a simple Gin and Tonic or an elaborate DuBarry cocktail, gin's delicate flavor asserts itself. It's a good spirit to experiment with.

GIN FLAVORS

Gin distillers call flavoring additives *botanicals,* because most are natural ingredients from plants. Each distiller carefully guards his company's secret formula for combining them.

The most important flavoring is juniper. Juniper berries come from bushy evergreen trees of the pine family. They grow wild in Europe and North America. Berries ripen every other year in fall or early winter. They are purplish-blue with a fresh-pine taste. In gin, their flavor always predominates, but other ingredients add underlying subtleties.

Coriander seeds contribute a spicy smell; angelica root adds musk. Cinnamon and dried orange contribute their own pleasant tastes. Other common gin additives include lemon, licorice and bitter almonds. Dutch gin (genever) uses caraway.

The appearance of the characteristic London dry gin came soon after the continuous still was invented. It made a pure spirit possible, encouraging dis-

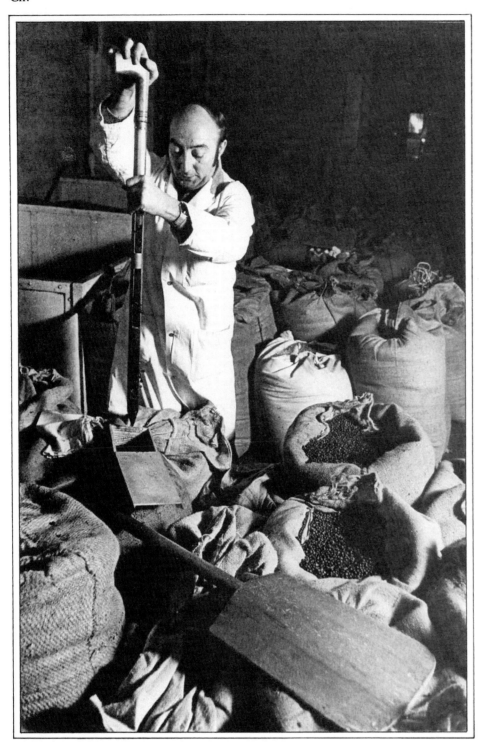

Taking a sample of juniper berries, one of the key ingredients of gin, at the London Gin distillery of Tanqueray, Gordon & Company Ltd.

HOW GIN IS MADE

Gin making is not dependent on any special climatic conditions or aging processes. Gin can be made from a variety of base spirits, including those produced from molasses and rice. Most English and American gins are distilled from a mash that's mostly composed of corn.

Distillation And Purification—After the cooked mash is fermented, it is distilled in a continuous still with at least three columns. The aim is to purify the spirit, leaving a totally neutral, flavorless alcohol. It is very strong when it comes out of the still—about 180 proof.

Adding Botanicals—The neutral spirit is placed in a pot still and re-distilled to add flavor. In the traditional method, the botanicals are mixed with the spirit. They are then re-distilled together. Some gin makers, however, hang the botanicals above the alcohol, where the rising vapor picks up flavors as it passes through them.

A faster method for adding botanicals is the *cold-mix system*. This involves steeping the flavoring elements in a small amount of neutral spirit, which is then distilled to give a powerful concentrated flavor, or *essence*. The essence is then blended with neutral alcohol to achieve the desired flavor. Some distillers export only the essences, which are blended into gin in the country in which they'll be sold.

If a label says *distilled gin*, the flavors were added in one of the ways just described. If it says *compound gin*, the oils of the botanicals were simply mixed with neutral spirits without re-distillation.

Aging—The United States doesn't allow any age claims on gin labels. In fact, gin doesn't require aging—you can drink it the day it's made. Some American companies age their gin in wood anyway, giving it a pale-gold color. This type of spirit is known as *golden gin*.

Bottling—Demineralized water may be added to the finished gin to reduce its alcoholic strength. It may also be filtered to remove any visible trace of botanicals. Traditionally, gin bottles

tillers to try an unsweet, or *dry*, style. Before, sweeteners were mainly used to mask unpleasant flavors in rough gins.

Although invented in England's capital city, London dry gin no longer has any specific geographical associations. Today it is made all over the globe. The expression basically refers to a gin that is tangy-dry and juniper-fresh.

are frosted glass, although this is less common today.

HOW TO SERVE GIN

Gins made in Holland, Belgium and Germany should be drunk straight and cold. This is because they are heavily flavored and full-bodied. Some people, however, mix these gins with bitters. Splash a few drops of any type of bitters in a small Old-Fashioned glass, rotate the glass until it's coated, then fill it with cold gin.

Some people say that having your gin in a Dry Martini is almost the same as drinking it straight. The Martini lover stoutly denies this, however, claiming that it takes skill to make the ideal version. Because the Dry Martini is so popular, it's given special attention on page 51.

Like the Martini, long drinks are particularly good when made with gin. Classic ones include the Collins, which most people make with commercially bottled mix. To make a homemade Collins, mix the juice of one lemon, 1 teaspoon sugar, a dash of Angostura bitters and a jigger of gin. Stir with ice cubes and add soda to fill a highball glass. Stir again and garnish with lemon and cherry.

The Tom Collins used to be made with sweetened Old Tom gin, but today it's always mixed with London dry gin. A rarer drink—the John Collins—is made with Dutch gin.

Gin and Tonic is another classic long drink, a crisp and refreshing cooler on a warm summer afternoon. It originated during the British rule of India, when quinine in tonic water was used as a protection against malaria. Modern bottled tonics contain considerably less quinine, but they still have a pleasant tang. Pour a jigger of gin into a highball glass, fill it with tonic water and garnish with a slice of lime.

A Gin Fizz makes a good long drink for brunch. Shake the juice of 1/2 lemon with 1/2 tablespoon of powdered sugar and 1 jigger of dry gin together with ice in a cocktail shaker. Pour into a highball glass, add club soda and garnish with fruit.

For a Cream Fizz, add a dash of fresh heavy cream to the cocktail shaker. For a Grand Royal Fizz, use the basic recipe with the cream but add two dashes of maraschino liqueur and the juice of 1/2 orange. Recipes for

Gin Fizzes are endless—don't be afraid to try your own varieties.

"Short" cocktails made with gin include the Gimlet, made with just gin and Rose's lime juice. To make a Bronx, shake an ice cube, 1 jigger of gin, 1/2 jigger dry vermouth, 1/2 jigger sweet vermouth and the juice of 1/4 orange. Add an egg white for frothiness, if desired. Strain and serve in a cocktail glass.

A favorite drink at bridge clubs is the delicate Pink Lady—1 jigger of gin, 3 dashes of grenadine and an egg

The distillation unit on the first floor of this Gilbey's distillery is over 100 years old.

white shaken with ice. Or serve a frosty Orange Blossom—1 jigger of gin, the juice of 1/2 orange and 1/2 teaspoon of sugar shaken with ice.

A Singapore Sling calls for 1 jigger each of gin, cherry brandy, Cointreau and lemon juice. Shake all of these ingredients together with ice and serve in a highball glass with fresh pineapple and a cherry.

LONDON DRY, PLYMOUTH & GENEVER GINS

Although all dry styles, these three gins have distinctive characteristics.

LONDON DRY GIN

This is the world's best-known type of gin. It's made in distilleries all over the world. Any company may make its own version—the term *London dry* refers only to style.

Gins labeled *London dry* are made in three ways. The first is distilled and bottled in Britain, then exported. Beefeater is a popular example of this type.

A second variety is made under license from a British distiller. The manufacturer must strictly adhere to the original British recipe. U.S.-made Gordon's is an example.

A third variety of London dry gin is not formulated to any specific recipe from a British distiller. Instead, it's a copy of the dry, juniper-flavored style. Mass-bottled, private-label brands are made this way.

Chain-store brands are fine for most long drinks. Dry Martinis call for a better-quality spirit, however. Here's is a list of some excellent London dry gins you might try.

Beefeater—From the House of Burrough in England, this gin was first sold in the early 1800s. The family company that makes it uses the traditional method of adding the botanicals, not the cold-mix system. This gives the gin a strong flavor. It is 94.6 proof.

Bombay—The premium brand of G&J Greenall, Ltd. It's made in England from a recipe dating from 1761 and has a very smooth taste.

Boodles—Another gin that's made in England. It's a crisp, dry drink that comes in an interesting bottle.

Booth's—The oldest British gin firm, which began distilling in 1740. Their finest London dry gin has a delightful tang. The London-bottled Booth's gin is House of Lords. The company also markets High & Dry, a very delicate style that's made in the United States.

Burnett's—Produced in the U.S. by the Seagram Corporation. Seagram also makes a brand under its own name and sells it well in the U.S. and Canada.

Gilbey's—Gilbey's is made in the United States by International Distillers and Vintners Ltd., another international corporation. It is second in popularity only to Gordon's.

Gordon's—For 165 years, this famous gin was made exclusively in London. But the demands for British gin during Prohibition meant a tremendous expansion of exports to the United States. Soon after Prohibition, a Gordon's distillery was built in America, where the original British recipe is followed to the letter. It's sold in a clear glass bottle with a juniper-berry design. In Britain, it is sold in a green bottle to prevent illegal exports. Gordon's has a clean, crisp taste that's excellent for Martinis.

Tanqueray—The company is now owned by Distillers Co. Ltd. Like its associated company, Gordon's, this top-quality gin is made in a traditional distillery at Finsbury, once a London health spa known for its pure water. Today the Tanqueray distillery uses water from local wells. Unlike Gordon's, this gin is not made under license abroad, making it an expensive brand. It's a very smooth, full-bodied gin.

PLYMOUTH GIN

Historically, this style is associated with the British Navy, which has sailors in the port of Plymouth. The story goes that a ship's surgeon mixed rose-colored Angostura Bitters with gin to make the medicinal effect of bitters more palatable. This was the birth of *Pink Gin*, still popular in England today.

The naval interest in gin led to the establishment of a distillery at Plymouth in 1793, which is the sole producer of this distinctive style. The local water is said to give the gin a particular flavor. It is known as a "soft" spirit, less noticeably dry than London gins. The label of Plymouth Gin bears a black friar, because the distillery was once a monastery.

Front row: G&J Original London Dry Gin; De Kuyper Geneva Gin.
Back Row: Gordon's Special Dry London Gin; Beefeater London Distilled Dry Gin; Gilbey's London Dry Gin.

GENEVER GIN

The flavor of Dutch gin is unique. The aroma is stronger than that of the London dry style, and it has a fuller bouquet.

Genever is traditionally associated with the town of Schiedam near Rotterdam. Schiedam is also a center for grain, a vital raw material in gin making.

Some people call Dutch gin *Schiedam gin,* while others turn the name *genever* into *Geneva.* The old word *Hollands* is also sometimes used for this type of spirit.

Genever gin is made with malted barley, together with equal parts of corn and rye. The blend of cereals is fermented and then distilled again in a pot still to produce a spirit called *moutwijn* (malt wine). Unlike London dry styles, which use base spirits of 180 proof or more, the malt wine in Genever gin comes out of the still at about 100 proof. Therefore, it's not completely purified of the flavorful congeners in the mash. This accounts for the full-bodied, malty taste.

Part of the *moutwijn* is re-distilled with botanicals, which include caraway. The resulting gin spirit is then blended with a varying amount of the *moutwijn* saved from the first distilling.

The gin blends are divided into two categories—*oude jenever* (old genever) or *jonge jenever* (young genever). The names do not have any particular age meaning, but relate to style. *Oude jenever* contains more *moutwijn* and is therefore more pungent. *Jonge jenever* is lighter and more popular.

Both types of Dutch gin are aged before they're bottled. Most producers offer both styles.

One of the best-known distillers is de Kuyper, the first gin maker to become established in Schiedam during the 16th century. Another famous producer, Bols, sells its Genever in attractive brown, cylindrical crock bottles. Two more top names in the Dutch gin world are Hasekamp and Kokma. This type of gin is especially popular in eastern Canada.

OTHER DRY GINS

Wacholder is the German equivalent of gin, made from a neutral spirit flavored with juniper. The best version of German gin is called *Steinhäger* and comes from the village of Steinhägen in Westphalia. This has a particularly strong flavor of juniper because it is distilled from the fermented juniper berries. It is often bottled in stoneware crock bottles.

Belgians make Jenever gin, which is similar to the Dutch variety. It is not produced in large quantities, or widely known abroad. Producers include Smeets and Fryns, both old established firms in Hasselt.

The Spanish are enthusiastic gin drinkers and produce their own versions of London dry, as well as making Gordon's gin under license.

GINS OF THE UNITED STATES

It would be wrong to consider the gin scene in the United States without a second mention of Gordon's and Gilbey's, two London dry gins that outsell all other brands in the United States. During Prohibition, these gins were bought in London and sent to Antwerp or Hamburg. Then, by way of Canada, Nassau or Newfoundland, they found their way into the U.S. Since those days, persistent advertising campaigns have kept them popular. Like other gins of British origin, they sell at proofs of 80 or more.

Gins from U.S. recipes are usually 80 proof. Their flavors are much lighter than those of their British counterparts. Besides Seagram's, top domestic brands include Calvert's, Fleischmann's, and Hiram Walker's. Schenley's sells an American gin at 90 proof, but it is typically light in flavor.

AUSTRALIAN GIN

The Australians have two favorite brands—Gilbey's and Vicker's. Vicker's gin is made locally by a company that is a subsidiary of the British Distillers Company, Ltd. Gilbey's is made to a British formula in Australian distilleries.

Other gins sold in Australia are imported from Britain. Gordon's gin is made under license in New Zealand.

FLAVORED GINS

Most gin-producing countries have a tradition of adding various flavors and colors to their gins. In America, orange, pineapple and mint are favorites. In all of these gins, however, juniper is still the predominant flavor.

Gordon's also makes gins flavored with orange and lemon, as does Mr. Boston. Citrus fruits are sometimes used to flavor Genever gins. The Dutch also like the flavor of black currants.

Sloe gin, by contrast, is not a gin at all—it is a sweetened cordial without a trace of juniper. The flavoring comes from the red *sloe*—the fruit of the blackthorn.

Many cocktails call for sloe gin, including the famous Sloe Gin Fizz. Mix the juice of 1 lemon with 1 teaspoon sugar and 1 jigger of sloe gin. Add ice and club soda in a highball glass.

THE MARTINI

This is the most famous cocktail in the world—entire books have been written about it. Controversy surrounds both its origins and recipe.

The earliest possible source for this drink was a *Martinez* cocktail, which appeared in a bartending book in the late 19th century. But many insist that this classic cocktail was first created around 1915 in the Knickerbocker Hotel in New York by a bartender named Martini. There is also some evidence that a vermouth salesman working for Martini & Rossi actually invented this drink.

Experts have similar debates concerning the correct proportions of gin and vermouth. Over the years the mix has become progressively drier, requiring a larger percentage of gin than vermouth in the blend. Before World War I, proportions were three to one, but today some people merely spray the glass with vermouth.

In any case, all Martini recipes call for a measure of ice-cold gin along with some dry vermouth. Stir the ingredients with ice and strain them into a stemmed cocktail glass. Or, if you're not a purist, serve your Martini on the rocks.

You can garnish this simple creation with a green olive or a lemon twist. A pearl onion turns the drink into a Gibson. But the essence of a Martini is its effect—dry, tangy and stimulating to the appetite.

Back row: Cork Dry Gin;
Gilbey's Dry Gin;
Schinkenhäger.
Front row: Martini Cocktail;
Hawker's Sloe Gin;
Gordon's Dry Gin.

Rum

Basically, rum is any alcoholic beverage distilled from the fermented juice of sugarcane, cane syrup or molasses. It was invented when Spanish settlers in the West Indies noticed that the molasses in their sugar factories was fermenting naturally. When they distilled the sticky stuff, they had a rich, pleasant beverage.

It was a strong, dark spirit often served hot by the fireside in Europe or aboard a ship traveling the high seas. This aromatic, heavy style is also made today. Recently, however, a modern, white style is becoming more popular. It is light in flavor and easy to mix into elegant, cool cocktails.

HISTORY

Sugarcane has flourished on Caribbean islands ever since Columbus carried cuttings from the Canary Islands to the West Indies in 1493. As early as the 16th century, it was being distilled into rum.

The history of early stills is lost among legends of swashbuckling pirates, who supposedly were behind many of these ventures. The huge modern distilleries of today seem impersonal compared with the romanticized illegal stills of yore. Some stubborn rebels still exist, though. Every island from Jamaica to Barbados has moonshine rum made in old copper pot stills.

By the 17th century, rum was well established in the New World and in Europe, both as a warming medicine and a social drink. Experts argue about how it got its name. Some say it derives from *rumbullion* or *rumbustion*, British slang describing the riotous conduct often caused by rum-induced drunkenness. Another theory holds that the Latin name for sugar, *saccharum*, may have been shortened to *rum*. Another explanation is that the name derives from the French *arome* (aroma), because of the pungent and scented flavor of the spirit.

Rum rapidly acquired many nicknames, such as "kill devil," a reference to the way rum was used by Caribbean islanders to drive away demons of sickness. One 17th-century account mentions ". . . rumbullion, alias kill-devil, and this is made of sugarcanes distilled into a hot, hellish and terrible liquor."

With the increased importance of British and French influence in the Caribbean, both rum and raw molasses became valuable exports to Europe and the North American colonies. Early North American settlers prized rum as a cheap commodity for medicinal purposes. Needless to say, they also found that it helped to relieve the hardships of a pioneer existence.

Before 1775, rum was a best seller in North America. Average annual consumption per person was no less than four gallons of rum. George Washington distributed free rum as part of his electoral campaign. After his historic ride, Paul Revere is said to have quaffed down two glasses of Medford rum before he felt able to speak.

Many early New England seagoers made fortunes in the notorious "Triangular Trade." They filled their holds with locally made rum and took it to Africa, where they traded it for natives. Sailing back across the hemisphere, they stopped in the Caribbean to sell the natives as slaves to work in the sugarcane fields. Their payment was raw molasses, which they took home to New England to be made into more rum. Then the vicious triangle would begin again.

Rum even played a part in stirring up the American Revolution. The British Government taxed molasses in addition to tea, and the Boston Tea Party was aimed at both of these taxes. During the Revolutionary War, the British naval blockade was often breached by ships running rum into the New England States—a foretaste of a similar bootlegging effort that would come during Prohibition.

The sugarcane planters of the 18th century were often enormously wealthy, living in great splendor on their Caribbean estates. Here is a description of a party held on one occasion: "A marble basin, built in the middle of the garden especially for the purpose, served as a bowl. Into it were poured 1,200 bottles of rum, 1,200 bottles of Malaga wine and 400 quarts of boiling water. Then 600 pounds of the best cane sugar and 200 powdered nutmegs were added. The juice of 2,600 lemons was squeezed into this liquor.

"Onto the surface was launched a handsome mahogany boat, piloted by a boy of 12. He rowed about a few moments, then coasted to the side and began to serve the assembled company of 600, which gradually drank up the ocean on which he floated."

Scene on a sugar plantation in the West Indies, from an engraving ca. 1900.

Modern Times—Today, rum is made not only in the Caribbean, but also in South American countries such as Guyana and Venezuela. The islands of Madagascar and Réunion off the coast

of Africa produce their own unique styles of this spirit, mainly for France. Batavia, on the island of Java in Indonesia, produces Batavia Arak, a dry, brandylike rum bottled in Holland. The United States, Mexico, Australia and many other counties also produce rums, chiefly for domestic consumption.

Oddly enough, rum cannot be made legally in England. Instead, many Jamaican rums are shipped there as new spirits and aged in wooden casks in bonded London warehouses. The damp climate helps to improve the flavor. When bottled, they are known as *London Dock* rums.

HOW RUM IS MADE

Sugarcane is the raw material for rum. This does not mean that the cane gives sweetness to the spirit. It gives a complex variety of flavors and essences called *congeners*. These natural flavorings also contribute to your headache should you overindulge in rum!

Extracting The Molasses—The great majority of rum is made from molasses, a dark, sticky byproduct of the sugar-making process. The exception to this rule is French *rhum* from Caribbean islands that were former French colonies. Their practice is to use all of the sugarcane juice, producing a distinctive rum used mainly for cooking.

In molasses making, sugarcane is chopped and crushed between rollers. Then the residue is crushed again. The extracted juice is warmed almost to boiling point, then cooled. This very dark sugar solution is treated with lime and heated again. On further cooling, the sugar separates in crystal form, leaving the molasses for use in rum making.

Fermentation—The thick, liquid molasses is diluted with water and allowed to ferment. Fermentation may take 24 hours for white rums or several days for darker, medium-bodied styles. For very dark rums, fermentation takes almost two weeks, and a substance called *dunder* is added to the mixture. This is the residue left in the still from a previous batch, similar to the old yeasts used to make sour-mash whiskeys.

Dunder is used mainly in Jamaica, one of the last traditional rum-producing islands. Although other islands have been making rum for hundreds of years, the process is modernized in many distilleries. Only a basic pure rum spirit is produced—flavorings are added later, as in compound gins.

Distillation—Dry, light rums are always produced in a continuous still. Distilling them to very high proofs eliminates the dark, strong-flavored congeners. Dark, pungent rums are traditionally made in a pot still and distilled to much lower proofs. This retains the rich flavors.

Like whiskey, rum is sometimes blended. Often, dark rums include both pot-still and continuous-still spirits in the blend.

Maturation—For white rum, plain-oak casks are used, giving some smoothness but little or no color. Charred-oak barrels are preferred for dark rums, such as traditional Jamaican styles. The spirit spends at least three years aging before bottling. Like many other alcoholic beverages, rum can be diluted with water to reach the required alcoholic strength. Caramel may also be added to intensify the color. U.S. regulations do not allow any reference to aging on rum labels.

HOW TO SERVE RUM

Rum is a spirit of dramatic contrasts. It's the smooth, white, 80-proof spirit that forms the base for the Daiquiri and other familiar modern cocktails. But it is also a heavy, dark, warming spirit that is sold at up to 151 proof. Be sure you know which style you are buying—the light style usually carries a white or silver label; the dark has a gold or amber one. A red label indicates the heaviest of all styles—a "liqueur" rum similar to a brandy.

For Cooking—Dark rums are most popular. They may be used in sauces, desserts, candies and for flaming a variety of foods. In France, rum constitutes a major part of all spirits sold, and much of this is used for gourmet cooking. A typical French addition to omelettes or meats is this rum-raisin sauce: Stir together in a saucepan 1 cup beef gravy, 1/2 cup raisins, 1 tablespoon currant jelly, 1/2 teaspoon vinegar and 3 tablespoons dark rum. Simmer for 10 minutes and serve hot.

Rum is even more popular with Caribbean cooks—banana recipes almost always call for it as an ingredient. These islanders also have an old tradition of drinking rum warm and straight, the best way to enjoy a fine dark variety. Serve it after dinner in a globe-shape brandy glass.

Mixed Rum Drinks—Caribbean islanders are also known to enjoy their rum in refreshing fruit punches. Planter's Punch is one of the oldest recipes, dating back to the 17th century. A traditional rhyme describes the drink this way: "One (measure) of sour (lime juice), two of sweet (sugar), three of strong (rum), four of weak (ice)." The classic mixture may be varied by adding orange, grapefruit, pineapple juice or even coconut milk. Dark rums are favored for this drink, and the red labels on such bottles often indicate that they are for Planter's Punch.

An almost identical drink using light rum is the delicious Daiquiri, named at the turn of the century after a Cuban iron mine. Shake 1 jigger of white rum, the juice of 1/2 lime and 1 teaspoon of sugar with cracked ice.

Strain into a cocktail glass. For a frozen Daiquiri, use the same ingredients with shaved ice and whirl them in a blender. In recent years, fresh-fruit Daiquiris have become popular. To make one, substitute 1/2 cup peeled fruit for the lime juice and 1/2 jigger of a liqueur based on the same fruit for the sugar.

In long drinks, rum is most popular with cola, served with a twist of lime. Some people drink it with soda water or orange juice.

Rum seems at its show-off best in tropical-type cocktails, such as the Piña Colada. Combine 2 jiggers of white rum and 3 tablespoons crushed

Serving a rum ration to sailors of the British Royal Navy at Portsmouth Barracks, 1933.

pineapple with 1 jigger prepared cream of coconut, or fresh coconut milk or meat. Blend with shaved ice and strain into a highball glass. Or, serve it in a pineapple or coconut husk, lavishly decorated with citrus fruit.

A Mai Tai is another potent South-Seas drink: To 1 jigger of white rum add 1/2 jigger each of dark rum, tequila, and Triple Sec. Put in 1 jigger of apricot brandy and 1 jigger of orange juice, then add 1 dash each of Angostura Bitters and orgeat. Two dashes of grenadine finish this elaborate cocktail. Blend with ice until smooth and serve as above.

A Zombie is named after the mythical "living dead" of islands such as Haiti. Combine 1 jigger each of white rum, dark rum and apricot brandy. Add 1/2 jigger each of lemon, pineapple and orange juice. Blend with ice and serve in the same way as a Mai Tai.

Cold-Weather Rum Drinks—Drinks like the Zombie are refreshing on a summer evening, but for a blustery winter night, nothing beats a hot rum drink. Dark, gold-label types are best in these drinks, but you can use a white rum if you prefer. For an Early American Rum Toddy, mix in a mug 1 jigger of rum, 1 teaspoon sugar, 1 slice lemon, 3 cloves, and 1/2 stick cinnamon. Fill with boiling water and stir.

Hot Buttered Rum calls for 1 jigger of rum, 1/2 teaspoon butter, 3 cloves and hot water or tea. Also, don't forget to add rum to your favorite eggnog for a Christmas-morning treat.

55

NAVAL RUM

Although the term *naval rum* has no legal meaning, for the British drinker it is a distinctive style. This is the traditional warming base for many a good hot *grog*—rum diluted with water.

HISTORY

For more than 300 years, the British Royal Navy dispensed a daily measure of a rum to the crews of their ships. Conditions aboard ship were tough and dirty, and the daily rum issue made life more bearable. In addition, there was always a double issue before battle—apparently a slightly intoxicated crew was all the more anxious for action. The main brand of this rum today is *Pusser's,* a corruption of *purser's.* In the United States, it is sold at 95.5 proof.

Ship's pursers first began dispensing a daily *tot* of rum to British sailors in 1665. It was offered as a substitute for beer, which would not store well in warm climates. Each tot was 2 British ounces, equivalent to 2-1/2 U.S. ounces. This was usually watered down or diluted with lime juice in an attempt to prevent scurvy. This is how the British sailors acquired their nickname "limeys," now applied generally to the British.

WHO MAKES IT

Naval rum comes from Guyana and Trinidad and is blended on the island of Tortola in the British Virgin Islands. Some is sold in attractive stoneware flagons decorated with scenes of naval life. Even a modern-day yachtsman may invite a friend to enjoy a grog made with the spirit that gave courage to sailors of old.

Grog was instituted in 1740 on the orders of Admiral Vernon, commander-in-chief of the British Navy in the West Indies. Noting that sailors were frequently drunk on duty, he resolved that to overcome "the ill consequences of stupefying their rational qualities, the daily allowance should be every day mixed with water." **Homemade Grog** — To make a modern version of ship's grog, mix 1 jigger of dark rum with 2 jiggers of cold water in a cocktail glass. Squeeze in the juice

of a fresh lime, then float the lime on top. Add ice if you want to.

Make a hearty hot version of grog by combining in a mug the juice of 1 lemon, 1/2 teaspoon sugar, 1 lemon slice, a strip of orange rind, 3 cloves and a jigger of dark rum. Fill the mug with boiling water and serve with a cinnamon-stick stirrer.

NAVAL RUM IN THE U.S.

Dark rum was not reserved just for British sailors. Settlers in North America also appreciated a heavy, rich type of rum. It was used to make many mixed drinks, including the Colonial Flip. This concoction was made in a large earthenware pitcher filled two-thirds with strong beer. It was sweetened with sugar or molasses, and 6 ounces of rum were added for spirit. The whole mixture was warmed with a red-hot iron poker used to stir the drink. A little ginger or nutmeg was sprinkled on top of this hearty beverage before it was quaffed down in earthenware mugs.

In Southern states, a favorite drink called *Bombo* was made with a measure of dark rum, sugar to taste and cool water. It was served with a sprinkling of nutmeg.

CARIBBEAN DARK RUM

Each Caribbean island has its own traditional rum style, and each rum label must specify the island on which it was made. So when you buy *Jamaican rum,* you can be sure that you're getting a spirit actually made there. Distillers elsewhere may not use a term such as *Jamaican-type rum* to describe a spirit that was not made on the island.

A pungent dark style of rum is most commonly associated with Jamaica, although most other rum-producing areas also distill dark rums. Jamaica was one of the very first commercial rum producers, and it is still known as the home of some of the world's finest.

As mentioned earlier, flavorful residue from a previous batch of distilled spirits, called *dunder,* contains many natural yeasts. It's added to the molasses, which ferments and is distilled to rum. The dunder is one reason Jamaican rums have special flavor. The taste is rich and buttery, with a strong molasses aroma. Traditional varieties are sold at 86 to 97 proof, and you'll occasionally find a potent 151 proof.

WHERE IT IS MADE

Myer's is by far the most popular Jamaican rum in the U.S., but Appleton's Jamaican is also enjoyed. Both brands are 80 proof.

Blue Anchor Navy Rum;
Lemon Hart Golden Rum;
Lamb's Navy Rum.

Dark rums from Haiti and Martinique are made from sugarcane juice, so are not as pungent as Jamaican rums. They are discussed with other French-island rums later in this section.

A very famous dark rum comes from Guyana in South America. Although technically not a Caribbean rum, its style is similar to Jamaican rum. It is called *Demeraran* rum, after the river where the sugarcane grows. Both continuous and pot stills are used to produce this fine dark rum, which is colored with caramel to a deep molasses color.

Gold-label rums of Cuba are not exported, but you can find similar spirits from Trinidad and Costa Rica in gourmet stores. Mt. Gay Barbados gold-label rum from the island of Barbados is commonly available.

Caribbean distillers famous for white-label rums will usually also offer a gold-label variety, although these rums are more medium-bodied than heavy. Top brands include Bacardi and Ronrico.

CARIBBEAN LIGHT RUM

You might think of white rum as something relatively new, an alternative to gin or vodka for cocktails. But this light-bodied drink has traditions, too. It has even become the favorite drink of some of the people who live on the islands where it is made. The delicate lightness of white rum is far more suited to a hot climate than the heavier, dark varieties.

HOW IT IS MADE

Light-bodied rums are a Cuban innovation dating back about 100 years. In general they are lower in proof than the heavier styles, and they're aged for considerably shorter times.

White rums are made by fermenting molasses and water with pure yeast for two to four days. This wash then goes into a complex continuous still with three or more connected columns. The distilled and rectified spirit comes out of the still at a high proof as a pure, refined product. In some distilleries, the spirit is reduced to a fairly low proof, and the rum is drawn off at about the correct strength for bottling.

WHO MAKES IT

Bacardi is tops in world sales of light rum. All over the world, people order Bacardi and Coke instead of the generic rum and Coke.

Bacardi is made in Puerto Rico, as are many other fine white rums. Puerto Rico's importance as an exporter to North America increased during World War II, when its distilleries were used to produce industrial alcohol. After the war, this tropical island began to supply a more pleasurable alcoholic product.

No discussion of Caribbean white rum would be complete without some of the colorful history of the Bacardi distillery. Although it is a giant company today, it began in 1862 as a small family business in Cuba.

The company's founder, Don Sacundo Bacardi y Maso, emigrated with his large family to Cuba from Spain. The distillery they established quickly became successful. By 1893, Bacardi rum was winning awards.

Around this time, a curious event made Bacardi the favorite rum of Spain. The young heir to the Spanish throne took ill with fever, and doctors feared for his life. When a dose of Bacardi dark rum was given to him, the child miraculously recovered. The grateful monarch granted the Bacardi Company the right to use the Royal Arms of Spain on bottle labels.

During the early 1900s, Don Sacundo's son, Don Emilio, became a major political leader in Cuba. The distillery continued to thrive under his guidance, and it began producing many styles of rum.

When the Cuban revolution forced the company to move to Puerto Rico in 1960, it continued to dominate the U.S. market. Bacardi distilleries were also built on Nassau to make rum for England and other parts of the world.

Bacardi Rums—Añejo is a very old, premium rum that comes in a flat-sided, flask-type bottle. It contrasts with the company's Castillo brand, which is light-bodied and relatively inexpensive.

For those who like strong rum cocktails, Bacardi sells a rum at 151 proof. This particular bottle has a warning that it should not be used for flaming foods. The high alcoholic content could set your dining room on fire!

Other Puerto Rican Rums—Ronrico and Don Q are two very popular Puerto Rican white rums. They are

sparkling clear, with a very light body and taste.

Other Caribbean Rums—In addition to Puerto Rico and Jamaica, white rums are made in Cuba, Barbados and Trinidad. Even Guyana makes a white rum that contrasts sharply with the rich Demeraran style.

On the island of Jamaica, Lemon Hart makes an 86-proof white rum. Appleton white rum, also from Jamaica, comes from a distillery founded in the 17th century. It's aged in uncharred-oak barrels for 4 to 20 years before it is bottled.

When light rums are aged in charred oak, they take on a natural pale-gold color from the wood. These are called *Golden Rums,* and they have a slightly more mellow taste than the clear-white varieties. The Captain

Santigo;
Bacardi White;
Bacardi Gold;
Appleton White;
Dry Cane Superior.

Morgan Puerto Rican distillery offers a golden rum containing a special blend of spices. It's rich but light, with a bouquet that suggests a cream sherry.

U.S. RUM

Rum was one of the first spirits to be made in the early days of colonial America. A distillery was established in the early 17th century by Willem Keift, a Dutchman who was director-general of the New Netherlands. It was located on Staten Island and supplied with molasses from the West Indies. Similar distilleries also existed in the Boston area at this time. New England rum is still made in Massachusetts today, but only by a few firms. Old Medford and Pilgrim's are well-known brands.

A few other "specialty" rums are produced in the United States, including a dark rum made from blackstrap molasses in the South. But by far the great majority of the rum consumed in the U.S. is imported.

Unlike inexpensive brands of bourbon, vodka and gin, even mass-bottled, private-label brands of rum are imported—usually from the Virgin Islands. This is because rum must be made from fermented sugarcane molasses. Sugarcane is not a major U.S. agricultural crop.

Some firms import rums that are actually aged and bottled in the Virgin Islands, but many private-label brands are imported as high-proof spirits in kegs and bottled in the U.S. Caramel and oak chips are used to give a semblance of age and color.

Inexpensive Virgin-Island imports are all light styles. If you're serving rum straight or on the rocks, these spirits are not appropriate. But they are excellent for mixing, especially in punches with strong flavors that mask the taste of the spirit.

OTHER RUMS

The French are among the world's most enthusiastic rum drinkers. They have a fierce loyalty to *rhum* styles made on islands that were once French colonies.

HAITI

This island, with its colorful tradition of voodoo rites, has become more significant in rum production since Cuba ceased its exports.

The sugarcane is grown in a sheltered, northern corner of the island. The cane is crushed, and the juice immediately distilled, without prior fermentation. Pot stills are used for a double distillation, in the manner of French cognac brandies. The pot still gives the rum added fragrance without producing too much alcohol.

From the first distillation comes a rough rum called *clairin,* used by the local people in rituals and offered to the spirit god. The second distillation gives true rum, aromatic and medium-bodied.

Most Haitian rum is exported to France. Some brands include Rhum Barbancourt, Rhum Nazon, Rhum Tesserot, Rhum Champion and Rhum Tropical.

MARTINIQUE

This island is the home of the rum company best known to all Frenchmen—Bardinet. The distillery is on the northwest side of the island. As in Haiti, the spirit is made from unfermented cane juice. The rum is shipped to Bordeaux in France in large metal containers. On arrival, it is transferred to wooden casks for aging. Styles sold by Bardinet include Old Nick, a white rum; Rhum Negrita, the favorite kitchen rum; and Très Vieux Dillon, a dark style.

Some French rum is sold immediately after distillation as *grappe blanche.*

This white rum is the heart of many powerful French rum punches. Ready-mixed Martinique Rum Punch is available in France under the Duquesne label. This company also produces a matured white rum, Grand Case. Rhum Clement is a rival company, making both white and dark styles. A very full-bodied dark style fermented with dunder is called Rhum St. James. It sells in the United States at 91 proof.

GUADELOUPE

There are no well-known rums from this island. Rum made here goes direct to France for maturation and bottling under importers' brand names.

SOUTH AMERICAN RUMS

In Brazil the national drink is *cachaca,* made from sugarcane. It is very dry and often sweetened with sugar syrup to make it more palatable. In Paraguay and Uruguay, people drink *caña,* another version of rum. The spirit is also made in Mexico, Venezuela and Colombia.

IN THE PACIFIC

Batavia Arak is a delicious rum from Java. A special river water is mixed with the molasses that forms the base of arak rum. Wild yeasts and rice go into the fermentation vats to add special flavor. The Dutch and Swedes favor this brandylike spirit for making punch.

Tondeña rum hails from the Philippines. This 86-proof spirit has won awards all over the world. Both of these brands are available.

Australians make their own rum in Queensland as a byproduct of the sugar-refining industry. The largest distilling company is the Colonial Sugar Refining Company. Generally, Australian rums are light-bodied and mellow.

Saint James Royal Ambré;
Saint James Impérial Blanc;
Rhum Negrita;
Old Nick Martinique;
Tropic Superior.

Brandy

Brandy is the spirit resulting from distillation of a fermented, fruit-based liquid, typically grape wine. It is an ancient drink with a long and colorful history. It is traditionally served after dinner, although its cheering warmth is also enjoyable at other times.

SOME HISTORY

Brandy's oldest use may be medicinal. Concentrated spirits of wine were used in ancient Greece and Rome both as an antiseptic and as a primitive anesthetic. Using brandy for social drinking did not occur until much later.

As early as the 13th century a kind of brandy was being made from wine in both Spain and Italy. The French didn't begin making this spirit until more than 100 years later.

There are different theories about how brandy came to be made in France. Some say that wine was distilled to produce a concentrated spirit that took less space on ships during export. Others say that in the mid-16th century, the French were greatly influenced by the Italians. And when Catherine de Medici of Italy married into the French royal family, she brought with her a taste for the

In the early days of Armagnac production, it was usual for the producers to use a travelling still. This particular model is on permanent display at the House of Janneau, established in 1851 and still run by the founding family.

brandy of her homeland. It may well have been Queen Catherine who encouraged the French to make their own brandy.

Most spirits called *brandy* are distilled from grape wine, but some are made from a mash of fresh fruits, such as plums, cherries or apples. These are described in a later section, as are the flavored brandies known as *cordials*.

The most famous of all grape-based brandies is unquestionably *cognac*, named after an ancient city in southwest France. A fine cognac brandy is a distiller's work of art—amber and mellow, with a delicate bouquet. Any brandy bearing the name *cognac* must come from the area surrounding Cognac. Thousands of farmers grow their own grapes, make their own wines and distill their own brandies in this famous and picturesque region.

Another well-known French brandy comes from the region of Armagnac, south of Cognac. Fine brandies are also made in other parts of the world, including Italy, Spain, Germany, California, Mexico, Australia and South Africa. Each of these areas is justly proud of its own versions.

The famous cognac producers Martell built this distillery at Gallienne in 1973.

HOW BRANDY IS MADE

Producing a top-quality brandy depends on many factors. These include the type of base wine and kind of still used. The distiller's skill and the wood aging also contribute to a brandy's unique characteristics. Local climatic conditions influence the brandy, because they affect the grape crop that eventually becomes the base wine.

Distillation—Cognac is made by the old copper pot-still method, which is time-consuming and difficult. The wine is poured into the still and heated. The resulting vapor is condensed and collected.

The process is complicated because only the middle, or *heart*, of the vapors are kept to become finished cognac. The rest are re-distilled with the next batch of wine. Repeated distillations end up in a single barrel of cognac. A few Italian brandies are made by a similarly complicated pot-still method.

However, most of the world's brandies are made in a continuous still. These may be small, single-column units like the traditional stills of Armagnac. Or, they may be huge, multicolumn machines designed for ultimate speed and efficiency.

Maturation—All good brandies need time to mature and develop their full flavors. New cognac, for example, is colorless and coppery-tasting due to the metal in the still. After years of aging in wooden casks, it becomes golden and mellow.

Caramel syrup is added to aged brandies to deepen their color. Most brands are blended with water and other brandy batches to achieve a certain basic flavor and taste.

Aroma is your best clue to a brandy's quality. After you've finished the contents of a glass, wipe it with a clean dry cloth. Sniff the cloth. If it smells like vanilla, your brandy is young and *raw*. If the scent is delicate and woody, you have a well-aged spirit. An easier test, of course, is with your pocketbook—aged brandies cost much more than young ones!

HOW TO SERVE BRANDY

There are three basic styles of grape brandy, and you'll want to serve each one slightly differently.

Liqueur Brandies—The word *liqueur* does not imply that these fine spirits have been sweetened or flavored—it tells you that they are the oldest and finest brandies you can buy. Although normally served after dinner as digestive drinks, they may also be served before dinner as *apértifs* to sharpen your appetite.

Always serve liqueur brandies straight—never with water or on the rocks. Serve them in a glass that is easy to hold in one hand. The traditional glass is a balloon-shaped *snifter*, but the French prefer a tulip-shaped goblet. They say that it allows you to appreciate the brandy's bouquet.

The gigantic "fish bowls" used to serve brandy in some restaurants can make the aromas fade rapidly in the glass. So does warming good brandy over a flame. The best way to warm a brandy is to revolve the glass slowly in the palm of your hand.

Medium-Style Brandies—These spirits are not as old as liqueur brandies, but they've undergone several years of wood aging. They have a mellow ripeness that allows you to serve them straight or mixed with water or soda. Because they have basic flavors—not subtle ones—you can mix them in cocktails without being concerned about masking any delicate essences. They are also great to cook with.

Young Brandies—In some ways, these inexpensive blends are your best buy. They are seldom aged more than two years, and their flavors are mainly due to added wood powders, sweetening agents and fruit extracts. Even so, they are strong, useful spirits that are wonderful for marinating meats or flaming desserts. Strongly flavored punches and mixed drinks also taste fine with this type of brandy.

Brandy Cocktails—Many delicious cocktails use brandy. A famous one is the Sidecar: a mixture of 1 jigger each of brandy, lemon juice and Cointreau. Another flavorful combination is the Stinger: 1 jigger each of brandy and white crème de menthe. A Brandy Sour is a jigger of brandy with the juice of half a lemon and 1/2 teaspoon sugar. The popular Brandy Alexander is a rich mixture of 1 jigger each of brandy, crème de cacao and heavy cream. Like most brandy-based cocktails, these should be shaken well with ice and strained into a cocktail glass.

FRENCH COGNAC

For some unknown reason, the Cognac region was among the last in France to begin distilling brandy. The rich, warm spirit was being made near the town or Armagnac as early as 1411, but production didn't seriously begin around Cognac until the 17th century.

Some historians believe that a bad grape harvest finally forced Cognac grape growers to distill mediocre, light-bodied wines into heartier and tastier brandy. These growers were fortunate to be located near a large port city, so the brandies they made could be easily shipped overseas. By the mid-18th century, large amounts of cognac were being exported to England and Scandinavia. About 50 years later, these fine brandies were being enjoyed all over Europe and America.

The Charente River flows through the Cognac region, connecting it to the Atlantic Ocean. It is a rolling, peaceful countryside, dotted with groves of trees. In the old days, some areas were heavily wooded, and the current names for the official divisions of the Cognac region reflect this.

The subregions of Cognac vary according to climate and soil. These factors affect the quality of the brandy that comes from each. Here are the seven subregions in order of quality of brandy produced: *Grand Champagne* (Large Meadow), *Petite Champagne* (Small Meadow), *Borderies* (Edges), *Fins Bois* (Fine Woods), *Bons Bois* (Good Woods), *Bois Ordinaires* (Ordinary Woods) and *Bois À Terroir* (Earth Woods).

By far the majority of cognac comes from the two Champagne subregions. If the label on a brandy says *Fine Champagne*, it means it was made in one of these areas. It has nothing to do with sparkling champagne wine, which is made in an area many miles west of Cognac.

Remember that cognac brandy is always blended, so a bottle that you buy may contain spirits made in several subregions. The "big three" distillers—Courvoisier, Hennessy and Martell—all emphasize that delicious cognacs are the result of different vineyards all over the district, not just those in the two champagne subregions.

If you visit France, be sure to take a tour of a large cognac distillery. Also try to see one of the traditional low-ceiling aging rooms and a cooperage, where the special Limoges-oak barrels are made.

THE STAR SYSTEM

A star on a brandy label was originally used by cognac makers to celebrate the sighting of Haley's Comet. This "Comet Year" happened to be an excellent one for brandy. Distillers intended to add another star for each fine year after that, but the system eventually became unwieldy and confusing.

Today the stars have no official meaning, but here is a brief guide to what they roughly signify: *One-* and *Two-Star* brandies are cheap cooking spirits that are probably less than one year old. You can't buy these cognacs in the United States. By law, French brandies must be at least two years old before they can enter the U.S.

A *Three-Star* cognac has usually aged about three years in wood. It is the basic "house" brandy of most distillers. A *Four-* or *Five-Star* cognac has aged much longer, but you will never know the exact number of years from the label—cognac makers are not allowed to make any written reference to aging.

NAPOLEON BRANDY

The name *Napoleon* on a label has nothing to do with the famous emperor. It indicates that the brandy is a premium blend that has been aged for many years. These fine old brandies make up a small part of the market, and they usually sell at about twice the price of ordinary Three-Star blends.

Some producers replace the word *Napoleon* with their own terms for this type of brandy—Martell's *Cordon Bleu* and Hennessy's *Bras d'Or* are examples.

EXTRA, EXTRA VIEILLE, GRANDE RESERVE

These French terms designate the scarcest and best cognacs. They are a distiller's "showpiece" brandies, aged from 50 to 100 years. Because of their complex flavors, they are prized by connoisseurs around the world.

WHAT THE INITIALS MEAN

Because most cognac is exported to English-speaking countries, the initials you see on cognac labels stand for English words, not French ones.

V.S. —Means *Very Special*. Brandies with this on the label are usually about five years old.

Martell;
Bisquit V.S.O.P.;
Hennessy;
Prince Hubert de Polignac.

V.S.O.P.—Stands for *Very Superior Old Pale*. It is a 10- to 15-year-old blend of fine quality.

V.O.—This simply means *Very Old*. It has a soft, woody flavor, and is aged a little longer than V.S.O.P. brandy.

X.O. Or X.X.O.—The brandy is the same as an Extra or Grande Reserve. It's probably at least 50 years old, very rare and expensive.

HOW COGNAC IS MADE

Every step in cognac making is strictly controlled by the French government; inspectors are always on hand during the distilling season. But a spirit of individuality thrives around Cognac, where thousands of small farmers produce their own brandies in ancient family-owned stills. The home-made cognac is often sold to a large export company, which ages and blends it to sell under its own famous label.

After cognac comes out of the pot still, the brandy is cut with water and aged in special oak barrels, which are made of wood mainly from the forests of Limoges. The brandy starts out in new barrels, then is transferred to old ones. To prevent a bitter wood taste, very old brandies are moved into large glass flasks for aging.

A few months before bottling, a cognac is blended and brought down to 80 proof with water. When the brandy is in the bottle, its aging process stops. Therefore, there is no reason to keep cognac for years and years—it will not improve in quality.

MAJOR COGNAC BRANDS

Here are a few selected brands of cognac. Other fine brands include Camus, Delamain, Denis-Mounie, Polignac, Salignac and Otard.

Bisquit—This widely available brandy comes in four styles: V.O. or Three-Star; V.S.O.P.; Napoleon; and Extra Vieille, an old, rare deluxe variety.

Courvoisier—It is promoted as the "brandy of Napoleon" with a silhouette of the emperor on the label. This company owns no vineyards or distilleries—it merely buys young brandies from independent producers and ages, blends and bottles them in a distinctive squat decanter. Its Napoleon-style blend is particularly full-bodied and pleasant.

Hennessy—Founded by a venturesome Irish soldier in 1765, this company still retains its family image despite huge worldwide sales. It produces a full range of styles, from a Three-Star Bras Arme to the fine and rare deluxe blend Paradis. Hennessy brandies are smooth and woody, with complex character.

Martell—One of the oldest Cognac houses, this family-run distillery was founded in 1715. Martell's V.S.O.P. is Medaillon, which is fruity and well balanced. Try this company's elegant Cordon Bleu for a Napoleon-style brandy with a complex flavor.

Rémy Martin—This firm dates back to 1724. Today it specializes in a V.S.O.P. Fine Champagne blend that is aged in very old oak. This company is unique in that it does not produce a Three-Star style.

FRENCH ARMAGNAC

Famous as the "brandy of the Musketeers," this pungent and powerful drink comes from the French province of Gascony. Because their vineyards were located near the Spanish border, wine makers in this region were among the first to learn the art of distillation from the Moors, rulers of Spain during the Middle Ages.

Some of the small distilleries in this pleasant province date back to the early 15th century. As in the Cognac area, many small farmers still make their own brandies to sell to larger companies.

Armagnac produces a distinctive type of brandy, but the influence of Cognac is also strong. In fact, some of the local firms are owned by Cognac companies. For example, Janneau is a branch of Martell, and Malliac is connected with Courvoisier.

Not long ago, most armagnac was shipped northward for blending with cognac, but this practice is no longer allowed. In 1909, the French government established Armagnac's status as an independent brandy-making region. Since that time it has achieved world recognition. Many connoisseurs prefer its robustness to the lighter, smoother flavor of cognac.

HOW IT IS MADE

The base wines distilled into armagnac brandy are produced in three subregions—*Bas* (Low) *Armagnac, Haut* (High) *Armagnac* and *Tenarèze. Bas Armagnac* has the best soil for growing grapes and gives fruity brandy with a characteristic scent of ripe plums.

A great deal of armagnac used to be made in travelling stills that moved from farm to farm in the late fall, after the grapes had been harvested and fermented. Today, most growers have their own distilleries or belong to cooperatives supervised by government inspectors.

The wine is distilled in a simple continuous still, called an *alambic armagnaçais*, rather than the type of pot still used in Cognac. Armagnac is distilled only once, so it has many earthy flavoring elements in the spirit.

Like cognac, armagnac gains much of its character during aging. It is matured in locally made black-oak casks. The quality of each brandy depends on the amount of time it spends in wood.

Three-Star armagnac must be at least 3 years old if it is be be exported. V.S.O.P. styles are between 4 and 10 years old. Brandies called *Extra, Napoleon* or *Hors d'Age* are between 15 and 25 years old.

Most armagnacs are blended from wines from all three subregions of the district. A few companies offer vintage bottles from a single year's production. These can be fascinating to taste.

Overall, the blend of brandies in a bottle of armagnac is older than the

blend in a bottle of cognac. They are much darker in color, and are sometimes sold at a higher proof.

Armagnacs are sold in two traditional types of bottles. One is flat-sided and oval with a long neck; the other is round and squat. Opague glass decorated with colorful labels is often used for both styles. Brands include Janneau, Larressingle, Marquis de Montesquiou, Mattiac, Prince de Chabot, Ryst and H.A. Sempé.

OTHER EUROPEAN BRANDY

Good cooks often keep a bottle of brandy in the kitchen for flaming and flavoring various dishes. A spirit well suited to this purpose is a grape brandy that is not from Cognac or Armagnac. In France, these brandies are

Back row: Gran Moscato Bocchino;
Veterano Brandy;
Boudier's Marc de Bourgogne.
Front row: Grand Armagnac Janneau;
Asbach Uralt;
Mariacron Very Special Brandy;
Armagnac Marquis de Montesquiou.

known as *fine* brandies, and they are commonly served with water. Typically, they are considerably less expensive than the products of the two famous brandy-making regions. St. Rémy is one brand that is commonly available in the United States.

MARC, OR POMACE BRANDY

Another type of French brandy is called *marc*. This spirit is made entirely from fermented leftovers—the stems, seeds, pulp and skins that remain after grapes are pressed for juice. Marc is distilled and matured in glass or wood. The finished brandy may be either clear or brown-colored. It has a strong, slightly oily flavor that some people find interesting.

Marc is labeled according to the area in which it is made. If from Burgundy, it is called *Marc de Bourgogne*, for example. This spirit from Burgundy, aged in oak for color and flavor, is the only marc that is readily available outside France.

Generally, brandy made from wine-

making leftovers is known as *pomace* brandy. In Spain it's called *aquardiente de orujo*, while in Germany it goes by the name *testerbrandwein*.

ITALY

Of all the countries in the world, Italy produces the most pomace brandy. There it is called *grappa*. Italian distillers age it in glass to make a crystal clear but oily type of spirit. More than 30 Italian distillers make grappa, and many consider it the national drink.

GERMANY

German brandies are unique because they're mainly made from base wines fermented in Mediterranean countries. They are shipped in railroad tank cars to Germany, where they are distilled into the brandy. German brandies are clean and light in body. The largest distiller is Eckes, which exports Cantré and Mariacron. A more expensive brand is Asbach-Uralt.

CALIFORNIA BRANDY

Three out of every four bottles of brandy consumed in the United States are produced domestically. Nearly all of this comes from the fertile central region of California. The total annual production of this area exceeds that of France.

In the 1700s, Spanish missionaries planted a bland grape they had brought from Mexico. They fermented these "Mission grapes" into harsh-tasting primitive wines. Distillation was an easy way to improve their flavor, so a mediocre California brandy was born. It was not until the mid-19th century, when growers began to plant European wine grapes, that local brandy became better.

At that time, French cognac was mainly made with Folle Blanche and Colombard grapes. These were the varieties chosen by California growers who wanted to make brandy. The wine they made from the grapes was distilled to become an acceptable spirit. In fact, when French vineyards were ravaged by pestilence during the 1880s, vast amounts of Califoria brandy were sent to Europe.

Both pot and continuous stills were used in California in the 19th century. But production techniques were not sophisticated, and the spirits were sometimes not aged correctly. Just as the distillers were becoming more experienced, a legislative blow devastated the young industry.

Prohibition idled distilleries all over central California. Many healthy vineyards were torn out and replaced with other crops. Not until post-World War II was the brandy industry robust again.

When the vineyards were replanted, Thompson Seedless and Flame Tokay grapes replaced French varieties. These are not only less expensive to grow, but their clean, fairly neutral tastes are perfect for the light, fruity brandies favored in the United States.

In 1971, the California Advisory Board was created to monitor quality standards. They declared that only brandy made in the state from locally grown grapes can be labeled *California Brandy*. Like cognac, this proud name has gained recognition all over the world.

HOW IT IS MADE

Most California brandy is made in gigantic continuous stills made of gleaming stainless steel. The two distilling columns rise to a height of more than 50 feet. These huge stills are capable of processing more than 1,000 gallons each hour.

A contrast to these immense machines can be found in a few local wineries, which produce small amounts of premium brandy in pot stills. Some of the big distilleries, such as Christian Brothers, also make special pot-still brandies for blending with their continuous-still products.

One column of the big continuous stills is designed for distilling. The other is for rectifying the spirit to eliminate most of the strong flavoring elements. More of these congeners are removed by distilling the spirit to a high proof. This is why California brandy has a lighter flavor and body than cognac.

The raw spirit is aged in oak barrels from Arkansas and Tennessee. Most distillers use new barrels, but some used charred bourbon casks to impart a slightly sharp aroma. All California brandy must be aged at least two years, but most of it actually spends more than four years in wood. Because these brandies are designed to be light, aging is not as important as it is for cognac.

Before bottling, most California brandy is blended with water, other batches of brandy and flavoring elements called *rectifying agents*. The latter range from simple sweeteners to prune juice and sherry wine. Rectifying agents may not make up more than 2.5% of the finished brandy. California brandy is almost always sold at 80 proof.

HOW TO SERVE IT

Because of its mellow lightness, premium California brandy is delightful for sipping straight from a snifter, as you would a cognac. But is also adapts itself easily to punches, cocktails and long drinks. Substitute it for whiskey in a Manhattan, or fix this luscious Grasshopper for an after-dinner treat: Combine 3/4 ounce each white crème de cacao, green crème de menthe and California brandy. Add 1 jigger of sweet cream, shake with ice and strain into a cocktail glass.

CALIFORNIA BRANDY MAKERS

The great majority of California brandy comes from less than 20 companies, including the following. Many large California wineries, such as Paul Masson, also make good brandies.

Almadén—This fine sipping brandy comes from one of California's largest winemakers. It is particularly popular in Western states.

California Wine Association—It used to be a cooperative, but now is a corporation headquartered in Delano. Its best-selling continuous-still brandies are Aristocrat and A.R. Morrow. Both come in 80- and 100-proof styles. A.R. Morrow Bottled-in-Bond is aged at least six years and has a nice woody flavor. Aristocrat is a younger, less-expensive brandy with a slightly sweeter taste.

Christian Brothers—The number-one selling brandy in the United States. It is made by an order of wine-making monks, who strictly control its quality.

De Kuyper—In addition to its popular conventional brandy, this company makes a wide range of flavored styles.

E.M.J.—A relatively inexpensive brand that makes fine, light-bodied drinks.

Lejon—A premium California brandy, Lejon has a warm, woody mellowness.

Top: Paul Masson;
Aristocrat;
A.R. Morrow.
Bottom: Coronet VSQ;
The Christian Brothers.

OTHER BRANDIES

Many people identify brandy with Europe and the U.S., but drinkers in other parts of the world enjoy their own domestic blends too.

AUSTRALIA

Although the Australians are popularly known as a nation of beer drinkers, they also produce some notable wines and brandies. They are chiefly made for the home market, but some are exported to other countries.

The first Australian brandies were made in South Australia to use up excess grape harvests near the Murray River. Shortly after, New South Wales joined South Australia as a brandy-making region.

Thompson Seedless is the preferred grape in distilleries around the Murray River. Both continuous and pot stills are used to make a blended style.

Other South Australian brandies are made in the Barossa Valley. Château Tanunda, Australia's leading brand, is a conventional blend of continuous- and pot-still spirits. But one brand—Kaiser Stuhl—is made in a pot still and aged in oak much longer than the two years required by Australian law. It's a powerful, straight brandy that's rare and expensive.

Most Australian brandies are slightly sweetened before bottling. To be called *Old* they must be aged for five years. To be called *Very Old* they must be aged 10 years. Old brands include Seppelt Great Western, St. Agnes, Remy and Hennessy. The last two are associated with French distilleries of the same names.

SOUTH AFRICA

The reputation of South African wines is high in many parts of the world. Few people, however, realize that many fine brandies are also made there.

The original brandies of South Africa were primitive pomace spirits made from the leftovers of wine making. They were distilled a single time in a pot still to make a raw-tasting brandy with a powerful aroma. The Dutch called this drink *Cape Smaak*, meaning *Cape Taste*. Englishmen turned it into *Cape Smoke*, and they still use this term today to describe inferior grades of South African brandy.

Native Africans didn't taste strong

alcohol until European settlers introduced them to it, but soon after they were making their own versions of Cape Smaak. In addition, they made Buchu brandy. This is ordinary grape brandy with an infusion of leaves from the Buchu plant. Buchu leaves are said to cure almost all ills—even today this brandy is made with a medicinal purpose in mind. Promoted as an aid to digestion, Buchu is made by several companies, including Bosman, Douglas Green, Huguenot Wine Farmers and Uniewyn.

South African brandy is distilled in pot stills similar to those of France's Cognac region. Production methods also resemble those used for making cognac. As in France, brandy making is strictly controlled by the government.

Maturation takes place in oak casks imported from Limoges, France. After aging for a minimum of three years, brandies are selected by the blender, who makes various grades to be bottled. The finished blend is usually a mixture of pot-still brandy and neutral spirits, with a minimum of 25% pot-still brandy required by law. Pure water is added to reduce the strength to 86 U.S. proof.

Paarl Five Star is the most popular South African brand. The blend contains at least half pot-still spirits, and it's aged for five years. Its heavy sweetness is due to the addition of cane syrup and wine.

Other important producers of South African Brandy include Gilbey-Santhagens, Castle, J. Sedgewick Taylor, Uniewyn, Bertrams and K.W.V., a large cooperative organization that makes both wine and brandy. Their finest brand is a 10-year-old, but they also offer other grades of brandy, including a Three-Star. Terms on South African labels closely resemble those used to categorize French brandies.

MEXICO

Wine made in Mexico is relatively light in flavor, mainly because of the kind of grapes that are grown. Old vineyards of bland-tasting Mission grapes are gradually being replaced by more flavorful varieties, but more than half of the wine produced in Mexico continues to be made into acceptable brandy. Much of this is exported to the U.S., where it is particularly popular in the Southwest. The leading brand is Presidente.

SOUTH AMERICA

Several South American brandies are made, but the only one with any sort of world reputation is *pisco*, a colorless and powerful Peruvian pomace brandy. Americans first became familiar with it when huge quantities were shipped to California during the Gold Rush.

The most popular brand today is Inca, which comes in a crock-type bottle shaped like an Inca head. This strong, oily spirit is generally served in a Pisco Sour, a cocktail that substitutes pisco for whiskey in the classic Whiskey Sour recipe.

KWV Brandy;
Oude Meester
Liqueur Brandy;
Inca Pisco.

Tequila

The popularity of this spirit outside of Mexico is relatively recent. Even in the United States, it wasn't well known until the 1970s. Like white rum and vodka, tequila gained its fame from a cocktail—the Margarita.

The origins of tequila can be traced to the Aztecs. They made a wine called *pulque* from the heart of the mezcal plant. When the Spaniards conquered Mexico, they applied the art of distilling to this native wine.

THE SOURCE OF TEQUILA

Mezcal is a kind of *agave*, a succulent that matures in 10 to 12 years. The pulpy, gray-blue leaves of the mezcal are sometimes 10 feet long. At maturity the plant almost looks like a gigantic tulip.

A spectacular 20- to 30-foot flower stalk grows out of the center of the plant before it finally dies, but tequila makers don't let this happen. Instead, they cut off the outer leaves to get to the heart of the plant, called the *piña* (pineapple). The spikey core resembles a huge pineapple and weighs from 75 to 150 pounds. It is filled with a sweet, sticky sap that would have nourished the giant stalk, had it been allowed to grow.

There are many species of mezcal plants. The best are called *blue agave*, and they are planted in great numbers by big distilleries around the towns of Tequila and Tepatitlán near Guadalajara in the state of Jalisco. Just as all cognac must come from the Cognac district of France, Mexican tequila must be made in this region to bear the name *tequila*.

HOW TEQUILA IS MADE

The agave pineapples are roughly chopped and steamed in an oven for up to 24 hours. This concentrates the sweet sap and turns the starch into sugar. The cooked pineapples are chopped and pressed to extract the juices, which are fermented for two days. A little fermented material from a previous batch always goes into the vat, much as dunder is used in making Jamaican rum.

Tequila is fermented twice in a copper pot still. It comes out at a powerful 104 to 106 proof. Clear tequila—known as *white* or *silver*—sometimes rests in large vats for a month before water is added to reduce it to 80 or 86 proof. It is then bottled on the spot or exported in bulk to be bottled later.

Some tequila varieties are aged in large oak vats for nine months or more. The resulting pale-yellow color gives them the name *gold*. The aging is not overseen by government inspectors, so some producers add caramel coloring to achieve the golden effect.

The very best tequila is called *añejo*, Spanish for *aged*. It usually spends at least three years aging in wooden casks, but seldom more. If tequila is aged more than 10 years, it becomes bitter.

Connoisseurs of añejo buy it for the same high price that they'd pay for a fine French cognac.

TEQUILA BRANDS

Tequila has a strong, herbal flavor and a slightly oily consistency. The spirit that is sold in Mexico is generally higher in proof and more pungent than the "mixable" tequilas made for export.

As already mentioned, many of the export styles are shipped in bulk to be mass-bottled under a private label. Others are marketed by a major liquor company such as Jim Beam, which sells Beamero Tequila. Good-selling brands bottled in Mexico include Two Fingers and Montezuma, but the great leaders of world tequila sales are the following:

José Cuervo—This company was founded in 1795 by José Cuervo, who made tequila under a grant from the king of Spain. White, gold and añejo styles are available. All are light-flavored and smooth.

Tequila Sauza—Second only to

Tequila Cuervo;
Gonzalez Old
Gold Tequila;
Gonzalez White
Tequila;
Sauza Tequila
(in front).

Cuervo in popularity, Sauza tequila was first made in 1873. It remains a family business with a reputation for using ultramodern methods of production. In flavor, it is somewhat stronger than Cuervo.

HOW TO SERVE TEQUILA

Añejo tequila should be served straight and chilled, or on the rocks with a little water. A traditional Mexican way to enjoy tequila is a bit more colorful and requires a little skill. Slice a lime, pour a chilled jigger of tequila, and sprinkle a little salt on the back of your hand. Lick the salt, down the tequila and then quickly suck the lime. To do this with one hand, hold the jigger between forefinger and thumb and the lime between middle and ring finger.

Tequila Cocktails—The Margarita cocktail combines the same tasty ingredients in a way that is easier to enjoy. Rub a stemmed cocktail glass with a wedge of lemon or lime, then dip it gently into a saucer of salt. Shake with ice the juice of 1/2 lemon or lime, 1 jigger of tequila and 1/2 ounce of Triple Sec or 1/2 teaspoon of sugar (optional). Strain into the prepared cocktail glass and sip your Margarita over the salty rim.

The Tequila Sunrise is a popular drink that originated in California. Stir 4 ounces of orange juice and 1 jigger of tequila over ice cubes in an Old-Fashioned glass. Add 1/2 jigger of grenadine and let it sink to the bottom. Stir gently to achieve a streaky red "sunrise" effect.

MEZCAL

This drink is not common outside Mexico, but some brands can be purchased in the United States. Mezcal is a clear, oily brandy distilled from the agave-heart wine called *pulque*. This is certainly the only brandy-like spirit that's traditionally bottled with an agave-root worm in the bottom! The worm is said to give strength to anyone brave enough to gulp it down.

73

Fruit Spirits

Most of these unusual spirits are distilled from a base of sweet fruits. But some countries make brandies from starchy vegetables too.

FRUIT BRANDIES

The French word for a brandy made from a fruit other than grapes is *eau de vie,* meaning *water of life.* These fiery spirits are clear and colorless like water. And, they contain no added sweeteners, as do the flavored and colored liqueurs sometimes called *fruit brandies.*

You can't buy many of these fragrant spirits outside of the areas in which they are made. But in France, Germany, Yugoslavia and Scandinavia, they are served with pride in many of the finest taverns and restaurants.

Visitors to Europe are often surprised when they are offered one of these crystal-clear drinks instead of a colorful flavored cordial. But their surprise usually turns to pleasure before their glasses are empty.

Each country's favorite type of fruit brandy depends on which wild and cultivated fruits grow best. Orchard varieties such as apples, plums, cherries and pears are popular with many brandy makers. But wild elderberries, currants, strawberries and raspberries are also used.

HOW FRUIT BRANDIES ARE MADE

There are two ways to make fruit spirits. The first is used for fruits with pits, such as cherries, peaches and plums. The fruits are mashed along with some of their pits, then fermented with yeast in large tubs. Unlike grapes, these fruits take a long time to ferment—weeks or months.

The fermented fruit is distilled twice in a copper pot still. The pot is placed in a water bath so the heating is gentle, similar to a double boiler. This keeps the flame from "cooking out" the delicate fruit flavor.

Fruits and berries without pits—called *stoneless*—are made into brandy in another way. Instead of being crushed and fermented, they are finely chopped and placed in pure grain alcohol. This mixture is then distilled in a pot still in a bath of water.

Fruit spirits are not usually aged in barrels, because the woody taste would interfere with the delicate aromas and flavors. If they are aged at all, they are put in large earthenware jugs for several years. In general, only stone-fruit spirits are aged.

HOW TO SERVE FRUIT BRANDIES

In Europe, these dry white spirits are served chilled in the manner of aquavit. But unlike aquavit, they should not be consumed in one gulp. Sip them slowly. To release flavors and aromas, swirl and savor them in a medium-size wineglass.

Fruit brandies are at their best after dinner to aid digestion. They are also delicious in cooking, for both flaming and flavoring.

CHERRY

These fruit spirits are popularly known by the German word for cherry—*kirsch.* In Europe, most of this delicious brandy comes from the regions where France, Germany and Switzerland meet. Alsace is the famous French kirsch district. In Germany it's the picturesque Black Forest. Switzerland makes a distinctive style of cherry brandy, but only in small quantities.

French kirsch is graded by law into the following categories: *Kirsch Pur,* a pure-cherry distillate; *Kirsch Commerce,* which has added alcohol; *Kirsch Fantaisie,* alcohol flavored with kirsch and other elements; and *Kirsch Artificiel,* which is grain alcohol flavored with artificial essences.

For cooking and mixed drinks, Fantaisie and Artificiel are fine. To savor the beauty of true kirsch, you should buy one of the top two grades.

In the United States, cordial makers such as De Kuyper and Heublein distill a kirsch-like spirit good both for cooking and drinking.

How To Serve It—Sip kirsch cold and straight, or use it to give a special cherry fragrance to cocktails such as the tangy Moonlight: Shake with ice 1 jigger of gin, the juice of 1/2 grapefruit, 1 jigger of white wine, and 1/2 jigger of kirsch. Garnish with thinly shaved grapefruit peel.

Bertrand Poire William;
Dettling Kirsch;
Bols Kirschwasser;
Boudier Eaux de Vie (Quetsch, Poire William, Kirsch, Prune, Framboise, Mirabelle).

BLUE PLUM

Slivovitz is the world's best-known plum spirit. It is made in Yugoslavia with special plums from trees that are at least 20 years old. The plums are fermented for three months, then distilled twice. Unlike most fruit brandies, this spirit is aged in wood for three to five years. It has a fine, golden color and a rich, spicy plum taste.

YELLOW PLUM

This spirit is made mainly in France, where it's called *Mirabelle*. Like Slivovitz, it is aged several years to give it a mellow smoothness. Look for this plum-scented spirit in gourmet stores under the brand names Jacobert and Dolfi.

PEAR

Because it's difficult to ferment mashed pears, brandies made from them are often very expensive. The best brand sold in the U.S. is the German brand Kammer.

In France, bottles of pear brandy are sometimes sold with a whole pear floating inside. This effect is accomplished by tying an empty bottle over a tiny young fruit and allowing it to mature "under glass."

RASPBERRY

This type of brandy, called *framboise* in France, is becoming more popular. It's delicate and fruity, with a delightful raspberry aroma. One good brand is Dolfi, from Strasbourg on the Rhine.

APPLE

Apple brandy is made in several parts of Europe and the United States. The most famous of all comes from Normandy, France.

Calvados—This delicious Norman apple brandy was created many centuries ago. Although current production is carefully controlled by the French government, much calvados continues to be made in small, family-owned stills.

Like Cognac and Armagnac, the Normandy calvados-making district is divided into several subregions. Of these, Pays d'Auge makes the best apple brandy. In Pays d'Auge, only pot stills are used. The spirit is matured in oak for three to ten years before blending and bottling. The youngest, called *vieux* (old), has usually been aged about three years. *V.O.* is at least four years old. *V.S.O.P.* and *Extra* are aged five years or longer.

Calvados is usually served at room temperature in France, but ice cubes are a pleasant addition when drinking it in warmer climates. The taste is tangy and powerful, with a strong apple aroma. Brands available in the U.S. include Père Magloire, Arc de Triomphe, Busnel and Morice.

Applejack—When settlers arrived in New England in the 17th century, they tried to grow hops for beer. Because

Laird's Applejack;
Calvados Boulard;
Sake Sakura-Masamune;
Sake Gekkeikan.

the hops did not thrive and apple trees did, the settlers began making apple-jack. Traders carried the spirit inland, where its potency earned it nicknames like "Jersey Lightning."

Today this time-honored apple brandy continues to be made in New England and eastern Canada. The brandy itself is made in a manner similar to that of calvados, but it is usually blended with more than 50% grain alcohol. As a result, it has a lighter flavor and aroma than the French brandy. Major brands are Laird and Spea.

VEGETABLE BRANDIES

A rare type of aquavit distilled entirely from fermented potatoes could be considered a vegetable brandy. So could mezcal, which is made from the pulpy heart of an agave.

Okolehao—One of the most interesting vegetable spirits is Hawaii's okolehao, nicknamed *oke*, and pronounced *oak*. This brandy is made on the Islands from the root of the sacred Ti plant.

Oke was first made in the late 18th century by an inventive fellow who fermented the Ti roots in the bottom of his canoe. He distilled the resulting mash in a homemade still that used a water-cooled gun barrel as a condensing coil.

Today okolehao is made in modern continuous stills. Like vodka, it is filtered through charcoal and bottled without aging. Although rarely available on the North American mainland, this spirit is becoming more and more popular in the state of Hawaii. Both natives and tourists drink it in exotic cocktails, but it is most often enjoyed in a frosty "Oke and Coke."

Rice Brandy—Another type of vegetable brandy is based on rice. China is the main producer of this type of spirit today, as it has been since ancient times.

Chinese rice brandy differs from *sake*, Japanese rice wine. Chinese rice brandy is actually distilled from a base of fermented rice in continuous and pot stills. Sake is made from rice that is merely steamed, fermented and filtered.

Because it is not distilled, sake is not technically a spirit. But it combines surprisingly well with true spirits in cocktails like the Sakini. Try this Oriental Martini by combining 1 part sake with 3 parts gin or vodka.

Liqueurs & Cordials

Liqueurs & Cordials

bouue z garder si de courbles z de salees z dautres manieres asses se ce nest por remouou maladies. mais se user les estuer siles amendero selonc les ensegnemens que nous deisines en le premiere partie. car por les ensegnemens que nous deisines fesismes la si nos en passerons briement. de viii

Ins si se drii sesie en mat res ma meros se sohe se sus cauce z selonc ce quil est nomaus z vies z tour soit ce que toutes manie res de vin escaufent selor na ture luuns plus li autres

A Cellarer from the Sloan manuscript, late 13th century.

In the United States, a drink must contain at least 2-1/2% sugar to qualify as a liqueur or cordial. However, many have much more. In fact, some sweeter versions have more than 35% sugar, so consider this when you're counting calories.

WHAT THE WORDS MEAN

Some people think that there is a difference between a liqueur and a cordial. In fact, the two words stand for the same thing—a sweetened alcoholic beverage made by mixing or redistilling spirits with various flavors and colors.

Liqueur is the word used by most Europeans, while many Americans prefer *cordial*. In England, some people use the word *cordial* to describe a nonalcoholic flavored and sweetened beverage, such as Rose's lime juice. This is not the custom elsewhere.

You might think that the word *cordial* is applied to these sweet drinks because they are served in a cordial, friendly atmosphere. Actually, the word is derived from the Latin stem *cor*, meaning *heart*. This reflects the medieval custom of serving cordials as medicines to stimulate the heart.

The French word *liqueur* also has a Latin stem—*liquefacere*, meaning *to melt* or *dissolve*. It describes the way in which flavors are subtly blended with the basic spirit to make a complex drink.

In this book, the words *liqueur* and *cordial* are used interchangeably to reflect each manufacturer's preference. Some companies even dispense with these two words altogether, preferring to describe their products with words like *essence, digestif, oil, balm* or *crème*.

ANCIENT TIMES

Recipes for making digestive liqueurs have been found in Egyptian tombs. Scrolls from classical Greece describe stomach-soothing alcoholic drinks. It was during the Middle Ages, however, that liqueurs became widely known.

Monks and alchemists distilled them in an atmosphere of magic, trying to discover an elixir of eternal life. Even though they never found this mystical potion, they did manufacture many delicious herbal beverages. Some of these are even used medicinally today.

During the terrifying Black Death that devastated Europe in the 14th century, liqueurs distilled by monks and nuns were dispensed as life-restoring remedies. Drinking them in years of health was a way of warding off sickness.

Medieval cooks used liqueurs as flavorings to mask the unappetizing aromas of spoiled meats and vegetables. Because of their built-in sweeteners, they were especially popular in custards and other desserts.

At banquets, peppermint liqueurs were stylish digestive drinks. Instead of sipping them from elegant tiny glasses, however, guests gulped them down in one big therapeutic dose to stave off the indigestion that almost always followed the courtly events.

THE RENAISSANCE

By the 15th century, Italians had become leading liqueur makers. Liqueurs were particularly popular with ladies, who used them for all kinds of purposes.

Women in childbirth found the medicinal herbs helpful, and the alcohol acted as a primitive anesthetic. Girls who wished to charm a lover would purchase a special aphrodisiac liqueur.

Women supervised the preparation of alcoholic drinks at home, and every noble had a small still. Each lady took pride in her own special recipes for perking up neutral spirits with new and fascinating flavors. Spices and fruits from the East or the New World were enjoyed. Rare ingredients such as oranges, chocolate, cinnamon and ginger were combined in a variety of ways to make delicious drinks.

When Catherine De Medici married Henry II of France, she brought the fashion of liqueur drinking to the French court. Queen Catherine was also skillful in the distillery, where she concocted drinks such as the French had never tasted before. These were not only sipped socially but were used as magical potions.

More than a century after Catherine, liqueurs were still an important part of French life. Louis the Great was a notorious overeater, and his personal physician had to invent new cordials to soothe the royal stomach. The king's favorite was called *Rossoli*. Its recipe included orange flowers, cinnamon and cloves, as does the Italian Rossoli liqueur you can buy today.

INDUSTRIAL ENGLAND

As life became more modern, afternoon tea came into vogue in England, and liqueurs were one of the delights of the table. Ladies sometimes sipped them to excess—in one stage comedy of the day, a bridegroom demands that his betrothed banish "all auxiliaries to the tea table, such as orange, brandy, cinnamon, citron and barbados waters, together with ratifia."

The last-mentioned liqueur supposedly got its name from the custom of using it to drink toasts upon ratification of a treaty. Many cordials went by the name *ratifia*, most of which used a red fruit as a basic coloring and flavoring agent.

During this period, many liqueurs became complicated, requiring as many as 50 ingredients. In contrast, others became less complex and heavy, relying mainly on a sweet fruit essence for flavoring. Ratifia is an example of the lighter style of drink.

EARLY AMERICA

North American settlers from Europe brought family recipes for liqueurs to the New World. The New England housewife was skilled in preparing medicinal cordials. She substituted native fruits such as chokecherries for ingredients in European formulas. Among her richer concoctions was a liqueur that included brandy, oranges, saffron, cloves, cinnamon, raisins and nutmeg—an effective warmer on a cold New England evening!

Cordials remained popular throughout the 19th century, playing a large role in domestic hospitality. No matter what time of day guests arrived, they were often greeted with a glass of sweet liqueur. After dinner, they relaxed with tea or coffee and a flavorful digestive cordial.

MODERN TIMES

During the Jazz Age, cordials suddenly become old fashioned when stylish flappers and their dates abandoned them for the cocktail. The "fuddy-duddy" image is a sharp contrast to the elegant reputation liqueurs have today.

The image change since the 1920s and 1930s has mainly been the result of public-relations efforts of various importers and distillers. In the 1960s for example, crème de menthe on the rocks was promoted as a fashionable drink. In the 1970s, Galliano popularized the Harvey Wallbanger: 1 ounce of vodka and 6 ounces of orange juice stirred over ice in a highball glass topped off, of course, with 1/2 ounce of floating Galliano liqueur.

Bartenders of the 1960s and 1970s also concocted a delectable array of cocktails based on the cordial called *Southern Comfort*. This 100-proof drink is an old-time New Orleans favorite that still appeals to modern tastes. Try it in a tasty Black Widow: 2 ounces of rum, 1 ounce of Southern Comfort, the juice of 1/2 lime and 1/2 teaspoon of sugar shaken with ice and strained into a cocktail glass. If you want a strong drink, make a Southern Comfort-and-Bourbon by combining equal parts of each spirit over ice in an Old-Fashioned glass.

Popular cordials like Galliano and Southern Comfort are associated with the sophisticated, modern drinker. But some older European liqueurs are still surrounded by an aura of ancient mystery. Many treasured recipes are privately passed down through generations. The formula for making Bénédictine D.O.M., for example, is never known to more than three people at one time.

Some of these special formulas are still guarded by monks who continue to make their liqueurs behind closed monastery doors. For example, Chartreuse has been made in France by the Order of Carthusian Fathers since the early 17th century. A subtle blend of 130 different herbs, this bracing elixir is similar to the medicinal liqueurs made in the Middle Ages.

TYPES AND BRANDS OF LIQUEURS

Some people think that basic flavor types such as crème de menthe are brand names. This is not so. In fact, any mint-flavored liqueur can be called *crème de menthe*.

However, some companies invent their own names for a specific flavor type. These names are owned by the company and can't be used by any other firm. Freezomint by Cusenier is an example.

Many *proprietary* styles of liqueurs are identified with a single manufacturer. Some have a monastic history, such as Bénédictine and Chartreuse. But sometimes these names designate a commercial style that has not been successfully duplicated by other makers. Irish Mist and Strega are examples.

Among European producers offering an extensive selection of liqueurs, several very old companies stand out. In France, Marie Brizard, Dolfi, Garnier, Rocher Frères, Regnier and Cusenier make a large variety of liqueurs for export. Some of these firms, such as Garnier and Regnier, also own liqueur plants in the United States, where different styles are made.

In Italy, the ancient brandy company Stock and the younger firm Galliano are best known for their products imported to the U.S. Gilka is a well-known German brand.

Holland is famous for the Bols distillery, which has been making fine liqueurs since the late 1600s. Bols also has plants in several countries, including the United States. Bols' liqueurs manufactured in the U.S. should be considered in a different category than Dutch-made Bols liqueurs.

In addition to Bols, leading U.S. cordial makers are De Kuyper, Leroux, Dubouchette, Dumont, Hiram Walker and Heublein's Arrow Brand. J.W. Dant and Mohawk also offer a variety of flavors. Don't be afraid to try domestic products—they might not be as strongly flavored as expensive imported brands, but you may prefer the lighter American style.

Distillery and warehouses of Joh's de Kuyper and Zoon at Schiedam, near Rotterdam, from an etching ca. 1800. Inset: De Kuyper's modern distillery at Cincinnati, Ohio.

How Liqueurs Are Made

Because of the wide variety of these beverages and the secrecy attached to their manufacture, it is hard to generalize about the ways they are made. However, all of them have some things in common.

THE SPIRIT BASE

The base of any liqueur is some sort of spirit. Usually, it is neutral, tasteless and very pure.

However, some liqueurs rely on the flavor of a particular spirit. Drambuie, for example, is based on Scotch; Irish Mist uses Irish whiskey.

Brandy is the heart of many top-quality French liqueurs such as Grand Marnier. The brandy used is never aged, because re-distilling it into a liqueur would destroy all of the complexities acquired by wood aging.

COLD METHODS

These three slow procedures are used to extract flavors from delicate fruits that might be damaged by heat.

Infusion—Fruits are crushed and left in cold water for up to a year. The liquid is then strained off and added to neutral alcohol.

Maceration—This is the same as infusion, except that the mashed fruits are soaked directly in pure alcohol. After filtration, the mass of remaining fruit is distilled in a pot still to extract all possible flavor and alcohol. The distilled alcohol is then mixed with the filtered batch.

Percolation—This type of cold method is laborious, but effective. The flavoring agent is placed in the upper part of a device that looks like a coffee percolator. The spirit is put in a container below and pumped, rather than boiled, through the flavoring ingredients. This goes on for weeks or months. In the end, the spirit-soaked flavoring agent is distilled to extract the last drop of flavor, and the two alcoholic liquids are blended.

HOT METHODS

The following procedures are much faster and more economical than cold methods.

Distillation In Alcohol—This is usually done in a small, copper pot still. The flavoring agent is soaked in alcohol for several hours, then put in the still with additional spirits. Only the middle part of the distilled liqueur is kept for use. The rest is re-distilled with the next batch.

Distillation In Water—The method is used for delicate herbs and flowers. They are soaked in water and distilled gently in a pot still that preserves their aromas. The flavored water is then added to pure alcohol.

COMPOUNDING

You can compare this procedure to the way spirits such as whiskey are blended. Many finished liqueurs contain elements that have been made by a variety of the hot and cold methods, along with neutral alcohol.

Compounding operations are extremely delicate because they determine the characteristics and quality of the finished liqueur. As in spirit making, water is often added to bring the product down in proof. Most liqueurs sell at 50 to 80 proof, although some, such as Green Chartreuse, are as strong as 110 proof.

When the alcoholic elements are compounded, sugar or another sweetener is added. Food coloring and herbal dyes are added to give the liqueur its characteristic color. Natural coloring agents include saffron, coffee, raspberries and currants.

Most liqueurs are filtered through charcoal or some other clarifying agent. Some of them "rest" in glass for a few weeks before bottling, but very few are aged.

HOW TO SERVE LIQUEURS

The simplest way to serve these delicious drinks is the oldest—pour a small amount in a tiny stemmed, crystal glass and sip it after dinner as a *digestif*. Miniature liqueur glasses come in many delightful and imaginative designs.

Coffee Drinks—Another after-dinner delight is liqueur-flavored coffee. Make Calypso Coffee with Tia Maria, Italian Coffee with Strega, Mexican Coffee with Kahlúa and Monk's Coffee with Bénédictine. All of these special coffees can be topped with freshly whipped cream.

Frappés—On a warm summer afternoon, liqueurs make delicious frappés. Pour your favorite variety over shaved ice in a small Old-Fashioned glass.

Cocktails—Liqueurs became popular cocktail ingredients during Prohibition because their sweet flavors smoothed the harshness of bootlegged spirits.

The easiest liqueur cocktails are made by merely floating the liqueur on top of another spirit.

Pousse-Café—Cordials float or sink relative to each other because they have different densities, or *specific gravities*. If you know the specific gravities of several liqueurs, you can create the Pousse-Café.

In France, a Pousse-Café is simply a cup of coffee with a float of liqueur on top. In the United States, it's a colorful combination of several chilled liqueurs floated on top of each other in a slender liqueur glass.

Some companies, such as Bols, list the specific gravities of their liqueurs on the label. The larger the number, the more the liqueur will sink.

To make a Pousse-Café, carefully pour each liqueur over the back of a spoon. Wait a few seconds for each layer to settle before pouring the next. You can keep these drinks in the refrigerator for as long as an hour before the layers begin to blend.

Here are two festive combinations: Red-white-and-blue for the Fourth of July—1 ounce each grenadine, Arrow crème de cacao and Arrow curaçao. Green-white-and-orange for St. Patrick's Day—1 ounce each crème de menthe, crème de cacao and peach liqueur.

CORDIALS IN THE KITCHEN

Fruit liqueurs are delicious sprinkled over grapefruit or added to a fresh-fruit cocktail. For a simple dessert, pour a chocolate, coffee or mint cordial over vanilla ice cream.

Many soufflés and mousses use liqueurs as flavoring agents. Some cordial makers offer free recipe booklets.

Even meat and egg dishes can be brightened up with liqueurs. For example, try glazing your turkey with Cointreau—an orange-flavored liqueur—for a gourmet Thanksgiving treat.

Cointreau is also the star ingredient in glamorous Crepes Suzette. Not only does it flavor the sauce, but it is also used to flambé the finished dish. To flambé a dish with a brandy or liqueur, warm the spirit gently for one minute in the pan and ignite it *carefully* with a match.

Carthusian monks produce Chartreuse. Here is Brother Marie Bernard holding samples of the very strong green liqueur and the sweeter, but less alcoholic, yellow liqueur.

Coffee, Chocolate & Other Favorite Liqueurs

As you read the following descriptions of basic liqueur types, remember that almost all of the major cordial manufacturers offer their own version of each flavor. Space limitations allow mentioning only the most popular and readily available brands.

COFFEE

The warm flavor of the coffee bean is the basis for some of the world's best-known liqueurs. These aromatic cordials sometimes go by the names *crème de café, mokka,* or *crème de mocha.*

Many American companies also make a coffee-based liqueur. One of them is Chase and Sanborn, the well-known coffee importer and distributor. This firm distills its liqueur in the U.S., but most other companies import it from Mexico. Sabroso marketed by Barton and Kamora sold by Jim Beam are two examples of relatively inexpensive Mexican imports.

Coffee-bean flavors are distinctive, and so are the liqueurs made from them. Italy's Stock Coffee Espresso is suggestive of sweet espresso; Pasha Turkish Coffee Liqueur reminds you of spicy Turkish coffee. Hawaiian coffee liqueurs—called *Kona*—are especially strong and sweet.

If you love Irish whiskey, you should try Gallwey's Irish Coffee Liqueur, which combines coffee-bean flavor with whiskey, honey and herbs. Sip it straight instead of adding it to coffee—it is fairly light in flavor.

The pungent taste of coffee blends well with many other flavors. Some delicious combinations include Mokka Mit Sahne, a German liqueur that incorporates cream; Kirsch Mit Mokka that blends coffee cordial and kirsch; and Ravanello that mixes coffee with vanilla. But the two most popular coffee liqueurs blend the bite of coffee with a slight flavor of chocolate:

Kahlúa—This is one of the top-selling liqueurs in the U.S. Distinctly heavy and sweet, it features the rich taste of strong Mexican coffee. You can also buy Kahlúa Black Russian, ready-mixed with vodka.

All Kahlúa sold in the U.S. is imported from Mexico, but in Europe it is made under license by the Peter Heering Company of Denmark. Similar Mexican brands include Kukul and Café Sonora.

Tia Maria—A drink that's dryer and lighter than Kahlúa. Company brochures say that it got its name from a servant woman named Tia Maria (Aunt Mary) who fled Jamaica with the Spaniards when the British took over the island. She brought with her a treasured family recipe for making coffee liqueur, and this recipe was supposedly rediscovered in recent years.

It is made with Jamaican Blue Mountain coffee extracts and has a delicate hint of chocolate flavor. Old Jamaica Blue Mountain Coffee Liqueur is a competing brand.

COFFEE LIQUEURS WITHOUT CHOCOLATE

Other coffee liqueurs include:

Bahai—A Brazilian liqueur made with local grain spirit and coffee. It is fairly light in flavor.

Bols Moccafé—A strong, pleasant blend with heavy body. It is medium-sweet.

Coffee Sport—Made by Jacquin and sold in a special heat-resistant decanter, which you can reuse for serving hot coffee.

Jameson's Irish Velvet—Produced by Irish Distillers of Dublin, this liqueur combines Jameson's Irish whiskey, coffee and sugar. It is specifically intended as a mixer for Irish coffee, not as a liqueur to be served alone.

Marie Brizard Café—Well-balanced and distinctive, this is one of the best liqueurs in this famous French producer's line.

Old Vienna Coffee Brandy—A Viennese coffee liqueur made by Meinl. It is stronger in flavor and alcoholic content than Kahlúa. Zwack is another brand with similar characteristics.

COCONUT

These smooth liqueurs have grown in popularity. Most of them use rum as a spirit base.

Some of the liqueurs blend coconut flavor with chocolate. Afri Koko from Sierra Leone in West Africa and Chococo from the Virgin Islands are examples, as is Arrow's Choclair, already mentioned. The Royal coconut-chocolate liqueur includes a small amount of milk to produce a caramel-like taste.

Coconut liqueurs that use only coconut for flavor are as smooth and white as cream. One popular brand—Cocoribe—is made in Ohio with coconuts and rum from the Virgin Islands. It is said to be inspired by the Caribbean tradition of a bridegroom offering his bride a coconut filled with rum.

Malibu is the British equivalent of Cocoribe, made with Jamaican rum and coconut. The makers recommend mixing it with Coca Cola or using it for exotic cocktails like the Caribbean Dawn: Combine 2 scoops of crushed ice, 2 jiggers of Malibu, 2 scoops of strawberry ice cream, 2 jiggers of Tequila and 2 dashes of strawberry syrup or liqueur. Whirl it in a blender for a short time, then pour into a large goblet and decorate with fresh strawberries. It serves two.

Tia Maria;
Kahlúa;
De Kuyper's Creme de Cafe;
Jameson's Irish Velvet;
Zwack Viennese Café.

CHOCOLATE

Chocolate has been popular in drinks for hundreds of years. At the palace of Montezuma, the explorer Cortez was entertained with delicious chocolate drinks, usually spiced and served warm.

Drinking chocolate spread to Spain during the 16th century, then to the rest of Europe. People thought that chocolate had aphrodisiac qualities and believed it to be an aid to digestion. Soon it became an important ingredient in various love potions and medicinal cordials.

The most familiar name for liqueurs made with chocolate is the French *crème de cacao*. This drink is usually colorless, but some manufacturers add coloring agents to make it a rich brown.

The basic flavoring ingredient of crème de cacao is always the cocoa bean. But almost all manufacturers blend these rich beans with a flavoring obtained from vanilla pods from West Africa or South America.

In the U.S., both Hiram Walker and Leroux make a wide range of cordials that combine chocolate with other flavors, such as cherry, banana, raspberry and mint. Arrow makes an interesting coconut-chocolate liqueur named Choclair. For a more exotic treat, try one of these brands:

Ashanti Gold—Produced by the Danish Peter Heering Company, best-known for its cherry brand, this liqueur is a rich, dark brown.

Bols Creme de Cacao—A delicious 50-proof liqueur that comes in both white and brown styles. The brown variety gets its color from percolation through the cocoa beans.

Chéri Suisse—Imported by the Seagram organization, this liqueur is attractively packaged in a ceramic bottle. It is flavored with cherries and chocolate. The company also makes Chocolat-Suisse, with small squares of Swiss chocolate floating in the bottle.

Chokalu—A chocolate liqueur from Mexico, the original home of the cocoa bean. If you see the name *Chouao* on the label, it means that the beans came from Venezuela, not Mexico.

Marie Brizard Crème de Cacao—It is flavored with a well-balanced blend of chocolate and vanilla.

Royal Chocolate Liqueurs—This line of liqueurs was developed in England by Hallgarten. Royal Mint-Chocolate was the first that appeared. Now you can buy other Royal-brand liqueurs that combine chocolate flavoring with orange, coffee, cherry, ginger, raspberry, lemon, and nuts.

Sabra—A delightful combination of bitter oranges and Swiss chocolate produced in Israel. Sold at 60 proof, it is rich and not too sugary.

Vandermint—A Dutch chocolate liqueur flavored with mint. It is sold in a pretty blue-and-white stoneware bottle.

NUTS

Almond is the most common nut flavor in liqueurs. The essence most often comes from almond oil or the edible nutlike kernel of fruit pits. Almond-flavored liqueurs are often sweet and pink in color. They go by the names *crème de almond*, *crème de noyaux*, *creme d'amandes* and *amaretto*. The last name is the most familiar to most people. Because it blends almond taste with apricot flavor, amaretto is discussed under Fruit Liqueurs.

In addition to almond liqueurs, there are several other nut varieties. Hawaii is the home of a macadamia-nut liqueur, and New Orleans prides itself on a rich praline-flavored cordial. Look for them in gourmet shops along with the varieties listed below:

Almendrado—A delightful product from the famous tequila maker José Cuervo, this light-flavored liqueur suggests the Mexican dessert almendrado.

Crème de Noisette—A liqueur made with hazelnuts. The French firm Meyer is a major producer. Each bottle contains a floating hazelnut.

Crème de Noix—A French liqueur made with walnuts from trees in Southwest France. The cordials are often made with young, green nuts. The liqueur is sometimes blended with one made from prunes, another local specialty.

Nocino—An Italian nut liqueur made by infusing various nut husks in spirit. Some Italian familes make their own nocino for cooking.

TEA

Tea used to be popular as a base for European liqueurs such as Marie Brizard's Tea Breeze, but today most tea-based cordials come from Japan.

Suntory Ocha Green Tea liqueur is best known. Both Matcha and Gyokuro teas are blended with grape brandy, and the liqueur is sold in attractive ceramic bottles. Though it has a pleasant "Oriental" flavor, it is also very sweet—almost 50% sugar. Because of its heavy sweetness, it does not appeal to most Western tastes.

A much lighter tea liqueur is Arrow Iced Tea cordial. Try adding it to a frosty glass of regular iced tea on a hot summer afternoon.

An unusual liqueur that suggests the flavor of sweet tea is actually made from maple syrup. The syrup is blended with brandy, and the mixture is allowed to "rest" for several months before sale. This maple liqueur is marketed by Rieder of Ontario, Canada.

Bols Creme de Cacao, light and dark; Royal Mint-Chocolate Liqueur.

PETER HALLGARTEN LIQUEURS Ltd BORDEAUX

Royal
Mint-Chocolate
Liqueur

PRODUCE OF FRANCE

CREAM

This category of liqueurs did not exist until recently. Of course, cream was an ingredient in many mixed drinks, including the Brandy Alexander, Grasshopper, White Russian and delicious Irish Coffee. But it was not until 1975 that R&A Bailey of Dublin perfected the technique of combining a liqueur with fresh Irish cream without souring the cream. The result was Bailey's Irish Cream.

At about the same time as Bailey's Irish Cream was introduced, Heublein began to sell Hereford Cows in the U.S. These drinks blend a variety of ingredients with milk. Mr. Boston makes a similar line, Aberdeen Cows.

Most cream-based liqueurs have relatively low alcoholic content. For example, Bailey's is only 34 proof. Although they can be enjoyed at any time, they are at their best after dinner. Serve them cold in well-chilled liqueur glasses.

These cream drinks are distinctly different from the traditional liqueurs called *crème*. Crème liqueurs do not include dairy products in their recipes.

Principal brands of cream-based liqueurs include the following:

American Cream—An imitation of Bailey's made by Heublein.

Bailey's Original Irish Cream—Irish exports of liqueurs to the U.S. rose by over 100% in a single year. And Original Irish Cream is the reason why. Its flavors are a rich blend of Irish whiskey and fresh cream, which is delivered daily to the Dublin plant that makes the liqueur. It is a pale-brown coffee color.

Carolan's Irish Cream Liqueur—This delicious blend is made in Tipperary. It is pink-brown in color and very creamy in taste. Honey is also used in the drink.

Chantré—A medium-brown blend of German brandy and cream with a strong brandy flavor. It makes a good after-dinner drink if you especially enjoy brandy.

Gaetano Creme Liqueur—Jim Beam makes this inexpensive American whiskey-and-cream drink.

Greensleeves—Made in London by John Dowland, it is a mixture of Devon cream, French brandy and English mint. It is pale green and has a soft mint flavor.

Heather Cream—A Scottish cream variety made with Bladnoch malt whisky, Scottish cream and sweetening.

Royal Tara Irish Cream Liqueur—Named after the seat of the ancient kings of Ireland in Cork, this sweet style of cream liqueur adds a hint of orange to Irish whiskey and cream.

Ryan's Irish Cream Liqueur—A low-proof liqueur that is fresh and light.

Waterford Cream—Slightly sharp in style, with strong whiskey flavor.

EGG

These liqueurs have two things in common with cream liqueurs. First, they have low alcoholic strength— usually 60 proof, as opposed to 80 proof for most spirits and cordials. Second, they may have a rich, creamy texture.

They are usually called *Egg Flip* or *Advocaat*. A Mexican version is called *Rompope*. Warninks Advocaat, a leading brand, is so popular that 60 million eggs are used in its making each year! Only the yolks are used. They are mixed with spirit and sugar, then blended to achieve a smooth, creamy look and consistency. Many consider the drink a health beverage.

Because Advocaat has the look and taste of a custard dessert, it is often used for mixing with fruit in a salad. In flavor, it is similar to eggnog.

Chantré Brandy Cream;
Warninks Advocaat;
Bols Advocaat;
Royal Tara Irish Cream Liqueur;
Waterford Cream;
Baileys Original Irish Cream.

Fruit Liqueurs

Many fruit liqueurs have long histories. While serious-minded monks were distilling brandy and adding herbs and spices to their medicinal drinks, distillers retained at court were busy experimenting with fruits. Their goal was to please the palate rather than to cure ills.

Imported fruits, such as oranges, were used in these early cordials. So was local farm produce in areas where a particular type of fruit flourished. To this day, various European regions are associated with certain fruits. The Burgundy region of France, for example, is famous not only for grapes, but also for black currants. These tasty fruits are the basis of a liqueur called *crème de cassis*.

In the U.S., fruit-flavored gins and vodkas are made by most cordial manufacturers. Originally, they were produced to get around state laws that banned the sale of any spirit but liqueurs in half-pint bottles. Today, they have become popular.

Typically, they contain only 2-1/2% sugar—just enough to qualify as a cordial. Popular flavors are cherry, lemon and lime. The taste is simple and reminiscent of hard candy. These drinks aren't comparable to complex liqueurs such as Peter Heering cherry brandy.

In addition to citrus fruits, many delicious liqueurs are made from fruits with pits, such as cherries, apricots, plums and peaches. Another group comes from soft berry fruits, including strawberries, raspberries, blackberries and currants.

Recently many liqueurs have been based on tropical fruits—such as pineapples, bananas, dates and passion fruits. And Suntory of Japan makes bright-green Midori melon liqueur that is growing in popularity.

Most European fruit cordials are made with fresh or dried fruits. In the U.S., most of the large firms use natural fruit concentrates or essences. A few use chemical flavorings, but this is not the general practice. All liqueurs using chemical flavors must say *imitation* or *artificial* on their labels.

FRUIT BRANDY OR FRUIT CORDIAL?

True fruit spirits or fruit brandies are dry and colorless. They were discussed earlier on pages 74 to 77. In the U.S., only this type of spirit may be labeled *fruit brandy*. Grape brandies that have been flavored with fruit concentrates must be called *fruit-flavored brandies*.

In Europe, things are not so simple, as the labeling of cherry brandy demonstrates. In Switzerland, a cherry brandy is based on kirsch. In England, however, it's a grape brandy flavored with cherries. In France, a cherry-flavored grape brandy is called *cherry liqueur*. If you're visiting Europe, be sure to look carefully at the description on the labels to make sure of what you're buying.

APRICOT

This aromatic fruit is perfect for making liqueurs, and most European and American manufacturers include an apricot cordial in their line. Most use grape brandy as the spirit base.

French brands include Abricotine from the house of Garnier, which has been making this cordial since 1859. Garnier apricot-flavored brandy made in the U.S. uses an imported French essence.

Marie Brizard makes Apry apricot liqueur, which also includes other fruits. Bols apricot brandy has herbs. Most U.S. makers use only apricots to flavor the brandy, so these are lighter and have less subtle flavors.

Apricot liqueurs, as with most fruit cordials, do not have a high alcohol content. This makes them good for mixing with stronger spirits to make a luscious cocktail. One of the most delicious is the Apricot Lady: Shake with ice 1 jigger of apricot brandy, 1 jigger of light rum, 1/2 ounce of curaçao, and 1/2 jigger of lime juice. Pour over ice cubes into a highball glass and garnish with a cherry and a fresh apricot slice.

Amaretto—This apricot liqueur is in a special category all its own. Its supporting flavor is bitter almond, which blends with the sweetness of apricots

Bols Apricot Brandy;
Zwack's Viennese Apricot;
Amaretto di Saronno.

to produce a special flavor that is a worldwide favorite.

Today almost every major liqueur manufacturer produces its own version of amaretto, but the best known is the original—Amaretto di Saronno from a small town in northwest Italy. It is made by a family that has been making liqueurs since the 18th century. Supposedly, it was invented by a young widow, who gave it to her lover to symbolize her affections.

Amaretto di Saronno is made from neutral alcohol, herbs and apricot pulp and kernels. Because the apricot is a relative of the almond, the seed imparts a strong almond taste. Amaretto del Orso and Galliano's Vaccari Amaretto are other Italian brands. All are rich and fruity, with a delightful almond bouquet.

CHERRY

These popular liqueurs can be made from any type of cherries—small, sour wild ones to large, sweet table fruits. Sometimes, the pits are included in the manufacturing process to give the liqueur a subtle almond flavor.

Cherry-flavored brandy is a special favorite in England. Like sloe gin, it is often offered as a morning "bracer" before a fox hunt. Guests in English country houses leave their hip flasks outside their bedroom doors at night to be filled with warming cherry cordial.

Well-known examples of cherry liqueurs include the following:

Bols Cherry Brandy—Bols makes a light-flavored version of cherry-flavored brandy and also makes a heavier maraschino style.

Buton Cherry Brandy—This Italian-made liqueur has a rich orange-red color and a bitter-almond flavor.

Cherry Marnier—A delicious full-bodied and sweet cherry drink from the company that makes Grand Marnier, an orange-flavored liqueur.

Cherry Rocher—A cherry liqueur made by Rocher Frères of France, founded in 1705. It uses cherries from all over France in its complex formula.

De Kuyper Cherry Brandy—The famous gin company based in Schiedam, Holland used to own the U.S. De Kuyper label, but this is no longer the case. Do not confuse U.S.-made De Kuyper cherry-flavored brandy with this European import. The European product is much more full-flavored and aromatic.

Grant's Cherry Brandy—Morella cherries grown in local orchards are blended with French brandy to make Grant's tawny-colored, smooth cordial. It is less sweet and heavy than most comparable European products.

Maraschino—It is not a brand name, but a flavor type named after the dark Marasca cherries used to make it. These are distilled several times, then the crushed pits and sweetening ingredients are added. The liqueur is either dark-red or clear. Maraschino is made mainly in Italy, and manufacturers include Drioli, Dolfi and Luxardo, all of whom package the richly aromatic drink in a straw-covered bottle. Stock also makes a delicious maraschino.

Try serving maraschino with tonic water in a highball glass filled with ice. Or mix it into this mild Diplomat Cocktail: Shake with ice 2 dashes maraschino liqueur, 2 jiggers dry vermouth and 1 jigger sweet vermouth. Strain into a cocktail glass and garnish with a cherry and lemon twist.

Peter Heering Liqueur—Formerly Cherry Heering, it was renamed after the founder of the firm, who began making cordials in 1818. He later developed large shipping interests to export his distinctive cherry liqueur all over the world.

The bright-red cherries used in Peter Heering are grown in southern Denmark, where the company has its distillery. The finished blend is

matured in huge oak vats. It is deep in color, with a tartness that comes from the fruit pits.

As with other cherry liqueurs, you can serve it straight in a chilled glass or in a variety of cocktails such as the Copenheering: Shake with ice 1-1/2 jiggers of Peter Heering liqueur with 1/2 jigger of gin. Strain into a cocktail glass and garnish with a cherry.

Sakura—Suntory of Japan makes this drink. Technically, it isn't a cherry liqueur because it is made with the blossoms, not the fruit, of cherry trees. It is pale pink in color and delicate in flavor.

PEACH

In general, peach liqueurs are not as rich in flavor as those made with apricots. Peach-kernel extracts are usually added for fuller flavor, and so is a fruit spirit distilled from peach purée.

European brands include Bols Peach Brandy and Marie Brizard Peach Liqueur, but the most famous drink using peaches in its complex flavor is the U.S.-made Southern Comfort.

Southern Comfort—Most people think that this cordial is based on bourbon whiskey, but the makers say that this is not so. Southern Comfort is made with a neutral spirit base and flavored with peach liqueur, together with fresh peach extracts and some citrus flavorings. It is aged in oak barrels for at least eight months before sale. The finished drink gives the impression of strong, sweetened bourbon.

It was first made around 1875 in New Orleans, where it was known as *Cuff and Buttons,* meaning *white tie and tails.* A St. Louis bartender coined the romantic name *Southern Comfort.* The recipe for this drink is still a well-guarded family secret, but the liqueur has several imitators. These include 100-proof Yukon Jack from Canada and 80-proof Laredo.

Southern Comfort comes in both 80- and 100-proof styles. It has a rich honey color and the aroma of herbs and fruit. Many delicious cocktails are based on it, including the Rhett Butler: Shake with ice 1 jigger Southern Comfort, 1 jigger orange curaçao and the juice of 1/2 lime. Strain into a highball glass over crushed ice.

The Southern Peach is a rich, creamy concoction: 1 jigger of Southern Comfort, 1 jigger of peach brandy, a dash of Angostura bitters and 1 jigger of heavy cream, all well-shaken with ice. Strain into a cocktail glass and garnish with a fresh peach slice and a fresh mint sprig.

De Kuyper Cherry Brandy;
Bols Cherry Brandy;
Southern Comfort;
Bols Peach Brandy;
Bols Maraschino;
Cherry Marnier.

CITRUS

Most citrus fruits originated in the Orient. Early explorers brought them back to Europe, and by the mid-16th century most monarchs had glassed-in *orangeries* attached to their palaces, where the trees could flourish.

In the New World, the Spanish planted citrus groves on the Caribbean islands, and later brought trees to Florida and California. Today, both bitter and sweet varieties are grown for making liqueurs.

Most citrus liqueurs are made from the peel of the fruit, not the pulp. This tradition goes back to the days when fresh fruit spoiled during long ocean voyages from the Far East. The dried peel shipped well and gave a strong, rich flavor to cordials. Today, the slight bitterness from the peel is a characteristic taste of citrus liqueurs.

There are two basic styles. The first is the full-flavored variety often called *curaçao*, after the former Dutch colony Curaçao. The second style is a drier liqueur called *triple sec* because of the three steps that go into the making. *Sec* means *dry* in French.

Triple Sec is usually clear, but curaçao is made in a range of colors, including dark orange, green and blue. Use the colored liqueurs to make novelty cocktails such as the Blue Angel: Shake with ice 1/2 jigger of blue curaçao, 1/2 jigger of parfait amour, 1 jigger of brandy, a dash of lemon juice and 1 jigger of heavy cream. Strain the startling blue mixture into a cocktail glass.

Well-known makers of curaçao include Marie Brizard, De Kuyper, Bols and Peter Heering. Germans make an *Apfelsinenlikoer,* a sweeter variety based on orange juice and cloves. But the two most famous names in the world of orange-flavored cordials are French:

Grand Marnier—This is still made by the Lapostolle family who introduced it to Europe about 100 years ago. To make the first Grand Marnier, Louis Alexandre Marnier-Lapostolle blended bitter Haitian oranges with fine French cognac from his family distillery.

Today there are two distinctive styles of Grand Marnier. The most expensive is *Cordon Rouge.* It closely duplicates the original recipe, with a cognac spirit base and a bitter orange flavor. Dark orange in color, it is aged in oak for at least 18 months.

Back row: Boudier Curaçao;
Mandarine Napoleon;
Bols Curaçao;
Bols Parfait Amour;
De Kuyper Blue Curaçao.

Forbidden Fruit—A traditional American whiskey-based liqueur using grapefruit, orange peel and honey. It is sold by Jacquin in a round bottle with an attractive filigree decoration.

Mandarine Napoléon—Said to have been created for one of Napoleon's mistresses, it is made by Pagès in Le Puy, France from tangerine peels that have been steeped in old brandies. It is light and dry in flavor because cognac is in the blend. The company also produces a fine *Grande Reserve* version with rare old cognac.

Mandarine Napoléon is useful both in the kitchen and behind the bar. Use it to make this interesting champagne cocktail: Fill a champagne glass 1/3 full of crushed ice, add 2 dashes of Angostura Bitters and 1 jigger of Mandarine Napoléon. Top with champagne and stir.

Parfait Amour—A very sweet liqueur based on citrus oils and flavored with essence of violets. Its color may be purple or deep red. In style, it is a relic of a few centuries past, when love-potion cordials were popular in Europe. Most U.S. liqueur makers offer a version of this antique drink.

Pimpeltjens—A traditional Dutch cordial made from lemons and oranges by De Kuyper of Holland. It is sold in an attractive blue-and-white crockery bottle.

Rock and Rye—This time-honored American cordial is made by steeping citrus fruits in rye whiskey. The first part of the name comes from the rock candy used for sweetening. Some brands, such as Donigan's, preserve the rock candy in crystal form. Leroux offers a rock and rye with floating pieces of fruit. Other popular brands are Arrow and De Kuyper.

The second style is Cordon Jaune. It is less expensive and pale in color because it does not use a brandy base. This is not sold in the U.S., so Grand Marnier you buy here will be the distinctive Cordon-Rouge style.

Cointreau—Grand Marnier is tops among darker orange liqueurs, but Cointreau is the king of the clear-colored triple secs. Most liqueur makers make their own version of this drink, but Cointreau continues to top sales chargs worldwide.

The French use it for cooking, especially for marinating fruits and other desserts. In the U.S., Cointreau is a versatile mixer in a wide variety of cocktails.

Cointreau is made with bitter orange peel from the West Indies and with sweet peel from Spain. It is double-distilled in copper pot stills and blended with sugar and water. The resulting drink is light and refreshing—a nice change from heavy, sweet cordials.

Other interesting citrus liqueurs include:

Arum—A pale-gold, brandy-based orange cordial from Italy.

Ben Shalom—Sweet Jaffa oranges are used in this Israeli liqueur.

Cayo Verde—A U.S.-made liqueur with limes and a neutral spirit base.

Dopio Cedro—This lemon-flavored Italian liqueur is made by Galliano.

Front row: Grand Marnier;
Oude Meester Van der Hum;
Hiram Walker Rock & Rye;
Pimpeltjens Nassau Orange Liqueur;
Cointreau (in front).

SOFT BERRIES

Black Currants—The most renowned liqueurs made with currants come from the Burgundy region of France. Black currants called *cassis* flourish there and are turned into excellent after-dinner drinks. Crème de cassis is often used to make Kir, a refreshing French drink: Add a dash of crème de cassis to champagne for a Kir Royale, or to burgundy wine for a Cardinal.

Well-known French brands include Garbriel Boudier, L'Heritier Boyot, Verdrènne and Lejay-Lagoute. Drink cassis within a year after opening the bottle because it tends to spoil.

Raspberry and Strawberry—As flavorings, these two berries are popular in France. Raspberry liqueurs are called *framboise*, and strawberry are fraise. In addition to the farm-grown berry liqueurs, there is an expensive *crème de fraises des boise*, made with wild strawberries. One brand is Sir Frederick's Wild Strawberry Brandy. Despite its English name, it is made in France from a 17th Century formula. Another good brand is Dolfi.

Cordial Campari is a strong, dry liqueur made with raspberries. Pour it over ice cream to make *gelato corretto*, a delicious Italian treat.

Blackberry—In the U.S., this deep-purple drink is the most popular of all flavored brandies. Almost every major liqueur house manufactures its own version. Many also offer blackberry liqueurs that use neutral spirits as the base.

OTHER FRUITS

Prunelle—Sloe gin, an American and English cordial, has already been mentioned several times in this book. Its unusual flavor comes from a blend of cherries and a wild purple plum called *prunelle*. With it, most U.S. liqueur makers make their own style of sloe gin.

Cranberry—Bogg's deep-red cranberry liqueur, made by Heublein, is a familiar sight on many American Thanksgiving tables. Regnier also makes a cranberry cordial called Cranberria. The Finnish version of this fruit liqueur is called *karp*.

Melon—Honeydew melons are the basis for Midori, an unusual Suntory liqueur. It is especially popular in Japan, where honeydews are considered

98

luxury fruits. In color, Midori is bright green, but no artificial flavorings are used in its making. Reishu is another brand of Japanese melon liqueur.

In Holland, Bols makes a pleasant melon cordial. In the U.S., you'll find Arrow honeydew melon liqueur and Kampai melon liqueur.

Use them in long drinks, such as the Midori Tropical: Mix 1 jigger of Midori with 2 jiggers each of orange and pineapple juice. For a stronger drink, mix equal parts of any melon liqueur and vodka. Top the spirits with lemonade or 7-Up to make a Moscow Melon.

Banana—Several countries produce their own versions of this bright yellow liqueur by macerating ripe bananas in pure spirit. The French have been making it for a long time, using bananas from Caribbean islands. The pungent aroma is sometimes overpowering, but banana cordials are excellent in desserts and mixed drinks if you use them sparingly.

Banana liqueur is a featured ingredient in a cocktail called *Silver Jubilee*. Shake with ice 1 jigger each of gin, heavy cream and crème de banana. Strain into a cocktail glass garnished with tropical fruit.

Pineapple—Most of these liqueurs are made in Hawaii. Their flavors are pungent and full. Arrow makes a piña colada liqueur that blends pineapple flavor with coconut.

Passion Fruit—A sweet, peach-like liqueur made from this fruit is another Hawaiian Island speciality.

Fig—Most countries that grow figs, especially Mediterranean nations, make their own version of this liqueur. It is rarely available outside of the producing area.

Prunelle Boudier;
Sisca Crème de Cassis;
Sir Frederick's Wild Strawberry Brandy;
Liqueur de Framboises;
Suntory Midori Melon Liqueur.

99

Herbal Liqueurs

These are the true descendants of the distilled potions that alchemists and early doctors believed had magical powers. In mysterious locked laboratories, the medieval counterparts of today's scientists labored to discover the secrets of life. Into their mixtures went rare and expensive elements such as gold mingled with ordinary garden herbs such as caraway. One 17th century liqueur recipe called for more than 100 ingredients, including such exotic imports as frankincense, amber and ground pearls.

In the apothecary room of many monasteries, scientifically minded monks collected and distilled equally rare ingredients. Some of their recipes have been passed down to us in monastic herbals handwritten on parchment.

Early American herbal liqueurs were often based on recipes from European monasteries, and this is still the case today. Claristine by Leroux, for example, is made from a formula originally developed by Belgian monks.

HOW HERBAL LIQUEURS ARE MADE

As with fruit liqueurs, most herbal cordials are based on a neutral spirit, usually made from sugar beets or grain. But a few use a more distinctive alcoholic base, notably Scotch or Irish whiskey. Some French producers include noticeable amounts of fine cognac or armagnac brandy in their liqueurs.

The herbal flavors are due to herbal essences extracted by maceration, percolation or distillation. Normally, the flavors are left to "marry" for some months in glass-lined vats or wooden barrels before bottling.

HOW TO SERVE HERBAL LIQUEURS

You can serve herbal drinks straight or use them in food or cocktail recipes. But in general, herbal liqueurs have strong flavors that you'll definitely notice in food or in mixed drinks. Use them sparingly so they don't overpower other flavors.

Many herbal liqueurs come in miniature bottles containing less than two ounces of spirit. This small amount is perfect for flavoring mixed drinks or adding to meat dishes or desserts.

Miniature bottles are particularly practical for herbal liqueurs, because these drinks can lose their subtle flavors when stored in unsealed bottles. A good rule is to never buy more herbal liqueur than you will use within a year.

In The Kitchen—The next time you have seafood, try perking it up with a sauce made with melted butter and several dashes of anise-flavored Pernod. Or, buy a miniature bottle of crème de menthe to add to a chocolate-cake mix. Dessert recipes using mint liqueurs are numerous, ranging from simple ice-cream sundaes to elaborately layered mousses.

At The Bar—To appreciate the subtle and complex nature of an herbal cordial, try each one straight at least once. Pour a bit into a small tulip-shaped goblet and sip slowly.

You can also enjoy any herbal cordial on the rocks or cold and straight in a chilled glass. Use a clear glass to avoid clouding the jewel-like beauty of these drinks. Cut or plain crystal glasses show them off at their glittering best.

Several cocktails call for herbal liqueurs, although usually as an accent rather than a major ingredient, for example as in the Harvey Wallbanger. B&B—half Bénédictine and half brandy—is such a popular cocktail that Bénédictine now markets it ready-mixed.

Green Chartreuse—one of the most strongly flavored herbal liqueurs—is an ingredient in the Spring-Feeling Cocktail: Shake with ice 1 jigger each of gin and Green Chartreuse along with the juice of 1/2 lemon. Strain into a cocktail glass.

Medicinal Uses—When you are sick, try using medicinal herbal liqueurs as they were originally intended. For example, add a jigger of Green Chartreuse to orange juice when you have a cold. Or, try a measure of Strega in a cup of hot tea to cure a headache.

The herbs in Pernod—anise, parsley, coriander and camomile—are well-known stomach soothers. Sip about an ounce from a small liqueur glass when you have indigestion.

HERBAL LIQUEURS BASED ON SCOTCH

Following the success of Drambuie, there are now several Scotch-based herbal liqueurs. The taste is best described as tangy, heathery and honey-smooth. Scotch-based liqueurs are delicious after-dinner drinks.

Drambuie—The name comes from the Celtic *an dram buidheach*, meaning *the drink that satisfies*. The recipe for this famous liqueur is said to have come from England's Bonnie Prince Charlie. After his army's defeat in 1746, he took refuge on the Scottish island of Skye, where he was cared for by a Captain MacKinnon. In gratitude, the prince gave the captain his own formula for a special Scotch liqueur.

The drink was made for family use until 1906, when an enterprising family member set up a commercial distillery in Edinburgh. Success was slow at first, but now the liqueur is known worldwide.

Glayva—This drink gets its name from the Celtic language—*gle nhath* means *very good*. First sold in 1947, it has a softer flavor than Drambuie, with anise undertones.

Glen Mist—This is produced by the House of Hallgarten, best known for Royal chocolate liqueurs. It is matured in whiskey casks for several months before sale.

Lochan Ora—Popular in the U.S., this Scotch-based liqueur is made by the producers of Chivas Regal and marketed by the Seagram corporation. It is light-bodied with a delicate herbal aroma.

Loch Lomond—This liqueur is made from a base of 12-year-old Scotches.

HERBAL LIQUEURS BASED ON OTHER SPIRITS

Scotch-based liqueurs lead the market, but other varieties, such as Irish Mist, are gaining in popularity.

Irish Whiskey—These rich liqueurs, like their Scotch-based cousins, are blended with herbs and honey. The best-known variety is Irish Mist, based on an ancient Irish recipe that was rediscovered in 1948. Mulligan's is an Irish Whiskey cordial that is flavored with fruits and herbs.

North American Whiskey—Yukon Jack has already been mentioned in the discussion of Southern Comfort. In addition to this brand, you can buy George M. Tiddy's Canadian liqueur, a tawny, medium-sweet herbal blend. Several bourbon-based cordials are made in the U.S., including Wild Turkey and Jeremiah Weed brands.

Brandy—Fruit-flavored cordials, such as Grand Marnier, using brandy as a spirit base have already been considered. So have flavored brandies such as the Greek Metaxa. In the pages that follow, more cordials based on brandy will be discussed, but the spirit itself is the main flavoring agent of only a few cordials.

French Sève Patricia is one brandy-dominated liqueur, as is the Italian Tulaca. If you visit Britain, try the Yorkshire specialty Brontë, named after the famous literary family. It is based on brandy, with added honey and herbs.

"MONASTERY-TYPE" HERBAL LIQUEURS

Even though some of these bracing drinks, such as Bénédictine, are no longer made by monks, the strong, complex herbal elixirs of France are commonly called "monastery-type" liqueurs.

Bénédictine D.O.M.—The initials stand for *Deo Optimo Maximo*, meaning *To God, most good, most great*. This amber drink is made according to an original recipe developed in 1510 at the Abbey of Fècamp. Probably the world's oldest continuously produced liqueur, Bénédictine is distilled in Normandy, France.

Even though the liqueur is now produced by a non-monastic corporation, the family that owns it still respects the drink's historical roots. When you visit Normandy, be sure to see Bénédictine being made at the beautiful gothic-style distillery. The building is a faithful duplicate of the original Abbey of Fècamp.

About 27 different herbs—including hyssop, angelica, coriander, nutmeg, thyme and cardamom—go into this delicious cordial. The herbs are combined into five special mixtures, which are matured separately in casks. Then they are blended with good-quality brandy to produce the finished Bénédictine.

The company's companion product B&B is drier and slightly stronger proof due to the addition of V.S.O.P. cognac.

Chartreuse—You can observe the making of this historic liqueur at Voiron, France. You have to watch the distillers at work behind a wall of glass because they are Carthusian monks sworn to silence and a life withdrawn from the world.

The recipe of Chartreuse has been a guarded secret for centuries. The recipe was first given to the monks in 1605 by a captain of the French King Henry IV. The recipe calls for 130 different herbs and several delicate stages of production. The finished liqueur is said to have the ability to prolong life and restore health. The taste is so subtle and complex that it is difficult to describe.

The original recipe is marketed today as Green Chartreuse. At 110 proof, it is more powerful than the honey-flavored, 80-proof yellow style. In Europe, Chartreuse Elixer Vegetal sells at 160 proof. It is classified as a pharmaceutical product and is taken in small doses for the common cold.

Izarra—Named from the Basque word for "star," this unusual French liqueur is made with fine armagnac brandy. It is flavored with rare flowers and herbs that grow in the foothills of the Pyrénées mountains. You can buy it in a 100-proof style or an 80-proof yellow style.

Trappistine—A Bénédictine-like amber liqueur made at the Abbey of Grace de Dieu in France from an old forumula using armagnac. Local mountain herbs lend their tastes to this powerful cordial.

Vieille Cure—Presented in a lovely bottle that resembles a stained-glass window, this aromatic liqueur is made at the Abbey of Cenons, not far from Bordeaux. It includes both cognac and armagnac, along with 52 herbs. Both

Molinari Sambuca; Galliano; Chartreuse; Bénédictine.

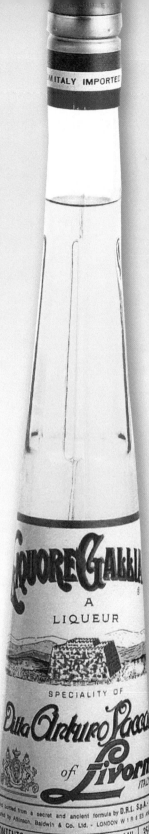

green and yellow styles are sold at 86 proof.

ITALIAN HERBAL LIQUEURS

Most Italian herbal liqueurs are similar to French yellow styles. They are honey-sweet and usually sold at 80 proof. Here are some examples:

Fior d'Alpi—Pale-yellow liqueurs made with herbs and flowers from the Italian Alps. They are packaged in tall white bottles. Inside each is a small twig covered with gleaming sugar crystals. Naturally, this makes the contents fragile and difficult to export. Recently, some manufacturers have begun using plastic twigs.

Galliano—This bright-yellow liqueur in a tall, tapered bottle is named after a military hero. The fort he defended in the late 19th century is still pictured on each Galliano label.

Today the liqueur is made by Riunite near Milan. The subtle blend of herbs and alcohol is stored in glass tanks for six months before bottling.

Strega—The name means *witch* in Italian, and this liqueur is reputed to be named after an ancient coven of witches who used to drink it as a love potion. More than 70 herbs are used in this drink, which is roughly similar to yellow Chartreuse.

Bitters

This category also includes descendants of the herbal medicines prepared by the apothecaries of old. Many people still use bitters medicinally because, among other things, they have a reputation for curing hangovers.

Bitters are closely related to liqueurs. Most of them are based on neutral spirits. They are flavored with herbs, roots and other aromatic ingredients, usually following an ancient recipe. All have a strong bitter flavor, and are usually sold at 80 or 90 proof.

In the U.S., bitters fall into two legal categories. The first is *medicinal*. They may not be sold in liquor stores—only in pharmacies. Although they may contain alcohol, they are exempt from liquor taxes. The second category is *nonmedicinal*. These drinks are taxed as are all alcoholic beverages, and you can buy them in liquor stores. Despite their classification as nonmedicinal, many have healing properties.

HOW TO SERVE BITTERS

Bitters can be served before of after dinner at room temperature in a small liqueur glass. Depending on the type, they will stimulate your appetite or aid your digestion. Another popular way of serving bitters is stirred with soda over ice cubes in a highball glass.

Many cocktail recipes call for a dash of bitters, but a few actually feature them as a main ingredient. When you're feeling queasy, try this Stomach Reviver cocktail: Shake with ice 1 jigger of brandy, 1/2 jigger of kümmel, 1 teaspoon of angostura bitters and 1 teaspoon Fernet Branca. Strain into a cocktail glass and serve without garnish.

TYPES AND BRANDS OF BITTERS

In addition to the brands mentioned below, many companies make their own versions of these styles. There are also orange and peach bitters that were once used to flavor gin.

Amer Picon—A French brand of bitters based on wine and brandy, usually served with ice and water.

Angostura Aromatic Bitters—Probably the world's best-known beverage flavoring of this type, it is called for in many cocktails. It was invented in Venezuela, but today it is made in Trinidad with a rum spirit base. *Angostura* is actually a brand name, and no other bitters maker has exactly copied its bright-red color and gentian-root

flavor. Use it in cocktails like the Old Fashioned, or add a few dashes to a bottle of gin to make it pink. You can also use these bitters to flavor sauces or salad dressings, especially if you're on a salt-free diet.

Boonekamp—This is the Dutch name for bitters. They are dark in color and include such ingredients as quinine, licorice and anise.

Campari Aperitivo—A brilliant red drink that is becoming a highly fashionable drink. It is especially popular with soda in a highball glass with ice. You can also serve it with orange juice or in many mixed drinks. In Europe, Campari comes ready-mixed with soda in miniature single-serving bottles. Thousands are sold every day.

Cynar—An unusual type of bitters

Ferro Chinar;
Angostura Bitters;
Fernet Branca Menta;
Unicum;
Fernet-Branca;
Campari.

from Italy that uses artichokes and various herbs for flavor.

Fernet Branca—Serve the renowned Italian medicinal drink mixed or alone. A companion product is flavored with mint.

Underberg—Made in Germany, this drink comes in miniature· bottles to drink as a quick pick-me-up. Serve it chilled in tiny glasses, like aquavit.

U.S.-Made Bitters—These are used in many cocktails. Abbott's Aged Bitters have been made by a family firm since 1865. Peychaud Bitters are from New Orleans, where they are used to flavor many local cocktails.

GENTIAN LIQUEURS

These drinks are popular mainly in France and Germany, where they are used to stimulate the appetite. The flavor is extracted from the root of the mountain gentian, and the resulting drink is earthy and bitter indeed.

The best-known brand is Suze, made by Pernod. It is a bright-yellow cordial in an attractive brown bottle. The taste is strong enough to put off any drinker who is unfamiliar with this type of beverage.

Cocktail Methods & Mixes

No one really knows how the cocktail got its name, but many people have theories. The most conservative say that it is an English garbling of a foreign word—Aztec, Spanish or French.

Others will tell you a colorful story like this one: In 1779, Betsy Flanagan, the pert Irish owner of a tavern near Yorktown, pilfered several roosters from a nearby Tory farm. Her tavern was a popular drinking spot with Washington's Yankee officers, and she did this deed on a dare from them. When she presented the officers with a stewed chicken dinner, each tankard that accompanied it was triumphantly decorated with one of the Tory cock's tail feathers—hence the name of the drink.

However the word originated, cocktails have been delighting people for many years. Today there are literally hundreds of varieties, all of which cool the fire of a spirit with wine, fruit juices or other mixers. *The Cocktail Book*, published by HPBooks, describes more than 200 delicious cocktails you can make with the spirits and liqueurs described in this book.

METHODS

A variety of cocktail recipes has been given, but it takes care and skill to prepare them in a way that is gracious and appealing.

BASIC BAR UTENSILS

In addition to the appropriate types of glasses, you'll need several bartending items. These include a 1-1/2 ounce jigger, a cocktail shaker, a stirring beaker and several corkscrews and bottle openers.

For mixing, you need a long-handled spoon and an electric blender. A wire-rimmed strainer with a handle lets you strain the shaken cocktail into the glass.

Ice Equipment—Three other basic needs are ice trays, an ice bucket and tongs. An ice shaver, an ice pick and an ice-crushing blender attachment are also handy items. If you don't have the blender attachment, you'll need a hammer to crush ice cubes wrapped in a folded cloth napkin.

Fruit Equipment—In addition to a hand or electric juicer, you will want a cutting board and a sharp stainless-steel knife. A small bowl covered with a damp napkin will keep garnishes fresh on your bar.

Serving Equipment—Straws, toothpicks, stirrers, cocktail napkins and coasters help make the drinks you serve look professional. Building your collection of bar accessories is part of the fun of mixing drinks.

SOME MIXING GUIDELINES

After you've mastered the art of expertly preparing a wide variety of standard cocktails, you might want to try inventing some of your own. Personal touches can be as simple as substituting your favorite spirit for the one called for in a drink recipe. Or your recipes can be as complex and original as you dare make them.

Even with your own recipes, be sure to stick to tried-and-true preparation methods. Don't be in doubt—measure with a jigger.

Stirring—For highballs, pour in the mix and then the spirit. Stir gently for about 15 seconds with a long-handled spoon. Clear drinks like the Martini should be stirred rather than shaken to preserve transparency.

Use a tall mixing beaker with a lip for pouring. Stir just until the glass begins to "sweat," then strain the drink into a cocktail glass.

Shaking—Shake your drinks vigorously with fresh ice until the shaker begins to feel frosty—never more. Remember that each ice cube is made of about 2 ounces of water. The longer it is shaken in a drink, the more water it will put into it. Overshaken or overstirred drinks taste lifeless and watery.

Blending—Elaborate tropical drinks and drinks to be served "frozen style" with crushed ice must be prepared in a blender. As in stirring and shaking, don't blend the drink any longer than necessary. Crushed or shaved ice works better than ice cubes, although cubes can be successfully used if you put an adequate amount of liquid in the blender jar.

MIXES

Fresh, home-prepared ingredients are always best, but sometimes you may choose prepared mixes for reasons of time and convenience.

NON-ALCOHOLIC COCKTAIL MIXES

Mixes come in many styles, including the ones below:

Sparkling Bottled Mixes—These are familiar to everyone. Collins mixes, tonic water and club soda are the most popular varieties. Make sure they are well-chilled before you use them, and always re-seal them tightly to preserve their carbonation.

Non-Sparkling Bottled And Canned Mixes—These products are formulated to make all types of cocktails, including the tropical varieties. Brands include Imperial, Ice Box, Rose's, La Paz, Mr. Boston, Trader Vic's and Tahiti Joe. Some are concentrates calling for dilution with water, but others need only the addition of a spirit. Be sure to read the instructions on the labels.

Dry Mixes—Three of the best known brands are Party Tyme, Bar-Tender's and Perfect Host. All offer a wide range of flavors, including exotics like the Strawberry Colada. These conveniently stored powders can taste surprisingly fresh, especially if you add a little freshly squeezed juice to the blend.

There are also crystalized types of drink mixes designed especially for use in a blender. True Crystals Peach Daiquiri is an example.

Frozen Mixes—Buy these in the juice section of your grocery store or in liquor shops. Daiquiri and Margarita mixes are the two most common types. Island Inn is a popular brand.

Batters—This style is usually reserved for buttery drinks. Trader Vic's Tom and Jerry and Hot Buttered Rum batters are examples.

PRE-MIXED ALCOHOLIC COCKTAILS

These cocktail mixes come complete with the spirit in the can or bottle. All you need do is shake them with ice or enjoy them on the rocks.

Common sizes are 6.8 ounces and 25.4 ounces. Look for the amount and brandname of the spirit on the label of each drink.

The Club, Heublein and Cocktails For Two are popular brands of pre-mixed cocktals. Enjoy them on the beach or on a picnic—they're the ultimate in drinking convenience!

Back row: Gimlet Mix;
Bloody Mary Mix;
Black Russian Mix.
Front row: Banana Colada Mix;
Pink Squirrel Cocktail Mix;
Grasshopper Cocktail Mix;
Cheri–Suisse Chocolate Liqueur;
Whiskey Sour Mix.

Index

Index

ACKNOWLEDGMENTS

I would like to thank the following individuals and organizations for their kind assistance in making this book:
Atkinson and Baldwin, London; Gabriel Boudier, Dijon, France; H.P. Bulmer, Hereford; James Burrough Ltd., London; Capital Wine & Travers Ltd., London; Cawardine's, London; Chinacraft Ltd., London; Nicholas Clarke, Henry C. Collison & Sons Ltd., London; Del Monico, London; Findlater Matta Agencies, London; The Glenlivet Distillers Ltd., Edinburgh; William Grant & Sons, London; Grants of St. James, Surrey; G&J. Greenall Ltd., Warrington; Gilbey Vintner's Ltd., Harlow Essex; Harrod's London; Hedges & Butler Ltd., London; Hiram Walker & Sons, London; Irish Distillers International Ltd., London; Matthew Clark & Sons Ltd., London; F&E May Ltd., London; Merrydown Wine Co. Ltd., Sussex; J.R. Parkington & Co. Ltd., Middlesex; Pimm's Ltd., London; R&C Vintners, Norwich; Saccone & Speed Ltd., Bucks; Stowells of Chelsea Ltd., Herts; Suntory UK Ltd., London; Wm. Teacher & Sons Ltd., Glasgow; Teltscher Bros. Ltd., London; United Rum Merchants Ltd., London; John Walker & Son, London; Whyte & Mackay Ltd., Glasgow.

Picture Credits:
BBC Hulton Picture Library, 8, 9, 29, 53, 55, 80-81; Whyte & Mackays, 14; Wm. Teacher & Sons Ltd., John Walker & Sons Ltd., 17; IDV, 34-37, 47; De Kuyper, 45, 83; DCL, 46; Janneau Armagnac, 62; Martell 63; Adam Woolfit/Susan Griggs, 85.